BASE 12 NUMEROLOGY

About the Author

Michael Smith is a numerologist and psychic medium who is fascinated with all things energy. Formerly an engineer and statistician, he offers mediumship, intuitive guidance, and base-12 numerology readings. His unique approach to numerology combines the power of ancient Pythagorean numerology with the cycles of twelve so prevalent in nature. Michael lives in Orton, Ontario, and can be found online at www.MichaelSmith12.com.

MICHAEL SMITH

BASE 12 NUMEROLOGY

Discover Your Life Path Through
Nature's Most Powerful Number

Llewellyn Publications
Woodbury, Minnesota

FIRST EDITION
First Printing, 2019

Cover design by Kevin R. Brown
Interior art provided by the author and the Llewellyn Art Department

Llewellyn Publications is a registered trademark of Llewellyn Worldwide Ltd.

Library of Congress Cataloging-in-Publication Data
Names: Smith, Michael (Psychic medium), author.
Title: Base-12 numerology : discover your life path through nature's most
    powerful number / Michael Smith.
Description: First edition. | Woodbury, Minnesota : Llewellyn Publications,
    2019. | Summary: "Michael Smith walks you through your own numerology
    reading and reveals how your days are full of vibrational potential and
    growth just waiting to be explored. Adapts traditional numerology to the
    cycles of twelve. Providing sample profiles, word meanings, and many
    clarifying examples and charts, this book makes it easy to put the
    numbers to work for you"— Provided by publisher.
Identifiers: LCCN 2019036684 (print) | LCCN 2019036685 (ebook) | ISBN
    9780738759371 (paperback) | ISBN 9780738761909 (ebook)
Subjects: LCSH: Numerology. | Duodecimal system—Miscellanea.
Classification: LCC BF1623.P9 S6155 2019 (print) | LCC BF1623.P9 (ebook)
    | DDC 133.3/35—dc23
LC record available at https://lccn.loc.gov/2019036684
LC ebook record available at https://lccn.loc.gov/2019036685

Llewellyn Publications
A Division of Llewellyn Worldwide Ltd.
2143 Wooddale Drive
Woodbury, MN 55125-2989
www.llewellyn.com

Printed in the United States of America

To everyone seeking answers to a number of questions
and to the twelve numbers that illuminate the way.

Contents

Acknowledgments

All my love goes to my wonderful wife, Teresa (life path 17/8, expression 12/3), whose unwavering encouragement (3) made this book possible. I am so grateful (8) we are on this journey (1) of spiritual truth (7) together. To my dear mother and father in spirit, Anne (life path 16/7) and Peter (life path 17/8), whose spiritual example and faith in me (7) enabled me to find my way here; my brothers in spirit, Colin (life path <u>11</u>) and David (life path master 11), for illuminating (<u>11</u>) my true self (11) through their timely visits to my dreams; and my siblings "on this side," Paula (life path 15/6), for her uplifting kindness (6), Mark (life path 13/4), for his grounded dependability (4), and Martin (life path 10/1), for his adventurous independence (1). Our paths complement each other in ways I appreciate more and more each day.

Special thanks to Heather Scavetta (life path 7, expression master 11), my spiritual teacher (7), who appeared when the student was ready, masterfully guiding me (11) through the confusing early days of developing my spiritual connection; and to all my fellow spiritual seekers, friends, and clients who have helped me more than you know.

My sincerest appreciation to Amy Glaser (current name 10/1) for giving me my start as a first-time author (1) and for seeing new beginnings (1) of potential (0) in this book and in me. To Lauryn Heineman (current name 13/4) for skillfully structuring my words (4) with positive (1) guidance and encouragement (3). Thanks to the entire team at Llewellyn (master number 33) for being the master catalyst and teacher (33) of spiritual empowerment for so many. You made my maiden voyage through the book publishing process a thoroughly enjoyable one.

INTRODUCTION

Every experience we encounter in life is a choice, a choice about how we will respond. Some of those choices are easy and others more difficult, but at the end of the day it is the sum of the many decisions we make that defines who we are and what we have learned.

Yet this is only half of the picture, the reactionary half: when stuff happens, we decide how to respond. The other part you may not realize is that everything you experience is also the result of your own choosing. That's because you energetically attracted those circumstances to yourself in the first place. Either consciously or more often subconsciously, what you choose to believe is what you project—and what you project is what you vibrationally attract. Maybe you disagree with that. Why would you possibly have chosen the various challenges, hardships, and heartbreaks you may have endured?

Nevertheless, science has proven that everything is energy in vibrational form. And a fundamental property of energy is that like vibrations naturally resonate with each other. In other words, like attracts like. So if we feel worthy and loving, we will attract situations and people that make us more abundant and loved, whereas if we feel undeserving and unlovable, we will attract more of the same. This is what numerology is all about.

Numerology is the ancient study of the energy of numbers. Every number has a vibrational personality, as does every letter based on its numerical position in the alphabet. When you add together the numbers in your birth date or the letters in your name, for instance, they combine into a distinct number vibration that you project as your personal "vibe."

In fact, your birth date and birth name set the vibrational theme for your life, the main lessons you are here to learn, and the talents, opportunities, and challenges that will help you explore them. These two key numbers reveal the vibrational path you chose for yourself before you incarnated into this physical experience and are the compass heading of your life. That's why your natal astrology chart also provides such an accurate reflection of your vibrational nature. It reveals the magnetic influence the solar system imprinted on you at your moment of birth. Your higher self or soul, the real "you," knows this and chose the time and place of your birth, as well as your name, to set your numerological compass needle just right. And you thought Mom and Dad did this all on their own!

The great news is that numerology provides a window into that vibrational world and is much easier to learn and apply than astrology. Not only does numerology decipher why you (and others) tend to act and react as you do, but also how you can steer through your vibrational journey with the greatest ease and joy. You can finally take control of your life, both personally and at work, and proactively navigate through each experience with confidence and grace.

Even better news is that the full power of numerology is finally unlocked through the base-12 vibrational language of nature. This book is the first to realign traditional base-10 numerology to the natural base-12 rhythm of the universe and provides profoundly greater accuracy and insight than ever before. This I believe is numerology as the Creative Source intended: as vibrational cycles of 12 harmonized through the 6 of love.

The purpose of this book is to empower you to master your vibrational life. I went from thinking my days were *numbered* and that life just happens to me to knowing that my days are *numbers*, full of vibrational potential and growth just waiting to be explored. Now you can too!

What Led Me to Base-12 Numerology?

A mechanical engineer and statistician by background, I spent the first thirty years of my working life in various manufacturing industries maximizing productivity and minimizing cost. I was your classic "numbers guy" and a die-hard skeptic of anything I couldn't see, touch, or count for myself. This included anything spiritual or metaphysical. I was reconciled to the notion that when I die, that was it. Curtains, nothingness, dust to dust. I didn't even remotely consider the possibility there could be life after death in any way, shape, or form.

That all changed in the fall of 2014 when I experienced a sudden spiritual awakening. This began with lucid dreams of loved ones who had passed and being woken by their voices calling my name and then quickly progressed to receiving clairvoyant messages while awake, including premonitions of events that would end up happening days later. This completely shook my worldview and challenged everything I thought I knew about life and death, so I went searching for answers.

Over the next couple of years, I explored a broad range of spiritual disciplines including meditation, psychic development, mediumship, channeling, energy healing, crystals, astrology and numerology. My mediumship abilities developed rapidly during this time and I eventually began offering readings professionally, leaving my manufacturing career behind. However, I also became particularly fascinated with numerology, prime numbers, and the base-12 number system for some reason. I had no idea what the connection could be between these three seemingly diverse areas of study but was pulled strongly in this direction nevertheless.

As a refresher from math class, a *prime number* is defined as any whole number greater than 1 that's only divisible by 1 and itself. Thus, the numbers 2, 3, 5, 7, 11, and 13 are the first handful of primes. Also, all possible whole numbers are either primes or products of primes. This is why prime numbers are often called the building blocks of mathematics.

Anyway, one day while playing around with base-12, I discovered a repeating vibrational pattern hidden within the prime numbers themselves. First, I found that the prime numbers, in addition to 1 but excluding 2 and 3, all seem to fall on the same four positions of the base-12 circle when viewed as a cycle. These four positions are 1, 5, 7, and <u>11</u>. Note that <u>11</u> is underlined here to distinguish it as a single digit in base-12 as opposed to the two-digit 11 we're used to in base-10. This is how we will denote the single-digit versions of <u>10</u> and <u>11</u> throughout the book from their double-digit counterparts.

When I then graphed rotations of those four positions as sine waves, it produced an elegant dual-wave pattern that repeats every twelve integers and looks just like the two-dimensional side view of the double-helix spiral of DNA. This is shown below as a pair of dashed and black overlapping waves, shifted sideways from each other but otherwise identical. Also, wherever these two waves intersect the horizontal number line (emphasized by dots) is where the prime numbers occur, again, along with 1 but excluding 2 and 3. I'll explain what's special about 1, 2, and 3 shortly.

Last, when I combined those two overlapping prime waves together, they produced the single perfect cosine wave shown in gray. This gray line appeared to represent the fundamental vibrational "chord" of the primes and the path along which each number's vibration achieves balance.

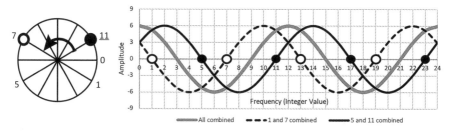

Base-12 Pattern of the Primes

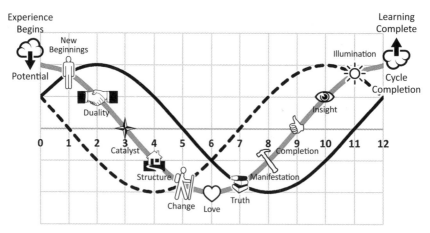

The Base-12 Numerology Cycle

I realized this dual waveform must be the fundamental structure of the prime numbers when numbers themselves are considered vibrational frequencies rather than just lifeless quantities. As that's exactly what numerology is, I was confident I had found the link between numerology, the primes, and base-12 that had been tugging on me.

Still, numerology takes it a step further by giving specific qualities or personalities to each number frequency within the cycle and to double-digit master numbers, such as 11, 22, and 33. These number definitions have stood the test of time, remaining unchanged over thousands of years. So, I wondered how the traditional base-10 number meanings might fit into the new base-12 pattern I had uncovered, if at all.

Sure enough, when I applied the traditional base-10 number definitions for 0 to 9 and master number 11 to the base-12 prime waveform, the geometry of the waveform at each number matched its number meaning perfectly. This not only validated the ancient number definitions from an objective mathematical perspective, but it also revealed to me that the true language of numerology has been base-12 all along.

More importantly, I now had a practical blueprint that explained everything about numerology in a single intuitive picture, a blueprint only brought into focus by switching from the base-10 lens to base-12. This included resolving some gaps and discrepancies within the base-10 approach, particularly concerning master numbers, that we will get to.

What convinced me to switch to base-12 most of all was how much more accurate and insightful my numerology readings were in base-12 than in base-10. I compared the back-to-back results for many individuals whose life stores and personalities I knew well, such as myself, family, friends, and famous celebrities. Base-12 simply provides superior results across the board, examples of which we will cover next in chapter 1, "Why Base-12?"

But the benefits of base-12 aren't limited to numerology alone. There are many ways in which base-12 outshines base-10. This should convince you, as it did me, that base-12 is the natural choice. Still, the real test will be by doing your own numerology reading both ways so that you can prove it to the person who knows you best—you! This book provides everything you will need to do just that.

So, despite the unexpected path that led me there, base-12 numerology was my destination. This prompted me to add base-12 numerology readings to my mediumship practice, and I haven't looked back since. Numerology has added a depth of understanding and a level of control to my life that has made everything so much easier and more fulfilling.

WHY BASE-12?

To answer that question, we need only look around us in daily life and in nature. Although you may not be aware of it, you are already very familiar with base-12 and rely on it in many important ways every day.

Following are some of the many advantages of base-12 that we will consider in this chapter, reinforcing why base-12 is an all-around better choice for numerology than base-10:

- Base-12 is more versatile and efficient than base-10.
- We already know and use base-12 in daily life.
- Astrology is in base-12.
- It's easy to count in base-12.
- Nature prefers base-12: in patterns of growth, the basic ingredients for life, the structure of DNA, and the subatomic world.
- Numerology readings are more accurate in base-12 than base-10.

Base-12 Is More Versatile and Efficient

The *decimal system*, or *base-10 number system*, as it is also known, is the predominant counting system in use today. Although there is some reasonable logic behind our modern adoption of base-10, particularly our having ten digits on our hands and mathematics seeming easier when working in tens, its usefulness for describing the real world is actually quite limited because of its poor divisibility.

The number 12 is an inherently versatile number mathematically because it's divisible by 2, 3, 4, and 6. This makes it twice as flexible and efficient than the number 10 of the traditional base-10 or decimal system, which is only divisible by 2 and 5. The number system that uses 12 as its base is called the *duodecimal, dozenal,* or *base-12 system* and was adopted by various earlier societies due to its well-recognized practicality for counting things and dividing them easily into equal groups.

Say, for example, you have 12 loaves of bread. You can divide them up evenly four different ways: in half (2 groups of 6 loaves), in thirds (3 groups of 4), in quarters (4 groups of 3) or in sixths (6 groups of 2). But if you only had 10 loaves, the best you could do is to divide them in half (2 groups of 5) or in fifths (5 groups of 2). After that, you're going to need a knife if you want to divide those 10 loaves up differently, and no one really wants the hassle and inefficiency of that.

This highlights how messy base-10 can get with all the extra fractions and decimal numbers caused by its poor divisibility. Dividing 10 loaves 4 ways, for example, would mean having to give each customer 10 / 4 = 2.5 loaves. Even worse is if you need to divide those same 10 loaves 3 ways (10 / 3 = 3.333...) or 6 ways (10 / 6 = 1.666...). A challenge for anyone's bread cutting skills.

Maybe that's why beer comes in cases of 6, 12, and 24. It's easier to keep track of getting your fair share, which is already harder to do if you like your beer. Um, so I'm told.

What's So Special about 1, 2 and 3?: Redefining the Prime Numbers in Base-12

This is as good a time as any to get this thorny question out of the way.

As mentioned in the introduction, the vibrational pattern of the primes is only apparent when viewed as cycles of 12 in base-12. Since the number 12 consists of the factors 2 and 3 (i.e., 2 x 2 x 3=12), the numbers 2 and 3 can be considered the underlying structure of the base-12 cycle itself, not of the primes generated by that cycle.

This is why primes can never occur at positions 2 or 3 of the base-12 cycle nor at any product that includes one or both of those numbers, such as 4 (2 x 2), 6 (2 x 3), 8 (2 x 2 x 2), 9 (3 x 3), 10 (2 x 5) or 10 (2 x 2 x 3). This leaves positions 1, 5, 7, and 11 as the only possible positions for primes to occur. This not only means that 2 and 3 should be *excluded* from the set of prime numbers, but also that 1 should be *included* since position 1 in the base-12 cycle is necessarily one of the four base-12 positions critical to the primes, contrary to the established definition of the prime numbers that excludes 1 but includes 2 and 3.

In fact, once we treat numbers as frequencies within vibrational cycles of 12 rather than just tick marks along a straight number line, the traditional definition of primes suddenly becomes obsolete and even misleading. Instead of being defined as "any whole number greater than 1 that's only divisible by 1 and itself," the base-10 definition of a prime number should actually be "1, 5, 7, or 11 or any multiple of 12 above each of these numbers that's only divisible by 1 and itself." That is, the first series of primes in base-10 are 1, 5, 7, 11, 1x12 + 1 = 13, 1x12 + 5 = 17, 1x12 + 7 = 19...and so on. Note that the first number disqualified as a prime under this new definition would be 2x12 + 1 = 25, since 25 is divisible by 5.

I know, sheer blasphemy to any mathematician reading this! Still, this is a hugely important argument to make as it is the key to unlocking the true nature of prime numbers as the *vibrational* building blocks of all numbers and not just the *numerical* building blocks. This therefore is also the key to understanding why numerology works and why we need to get this under our belts at this early point in the book.

This cyclical nature of numbers is not unique to base-12, by the way. It is also present in the base-10 number system. However, instead of 2 and 3 being the underlying structure of the cycle as in base-12, it is 2 and 5 (since 2 x 5 = 10). As such, primes can never occur at position 2 or 5 in the base-10 cycle nor at any product that includes one or both of those numbers, such as 4 (2 x 2), 6

(2 x 3), 8 (2 x 2 x 2) or 10 (2 x 5). This leaves positions 1, 3, 7, and 9 as the only possible positions for primes to occur in base-10. Once again, we see the 1 as a necessary "cyclical" factor of the primes.

The important difference between base-10 and base-12 when viewed as cycles, however, is that the four prime positions in base-12 possess a balanced rotational geometry, whereas in base-10 they do not, as illustrated below.

In base-12, the four prime positions create a symmetric rectangular geometry that, when expressed as vibrational sine waves, reduces to the two balanced waves of the base-12 numerology cycle. This is because the 1 and 7 positions are opposite each other on the base-12 circle, as are 5 and 11, such that each pair subtracts and combines to a single wave of amplitude 6 (7 – 1 = 6, 11 – 5 = 6).

In base-10, there's no such symmetry or combining of opposite frequencies. Instead, the four positions remain as separate sine waves of varying amplitude of 1, 3, 7 and 9 when graphed. The resulting combined waveform is a vibrational mess with no apparent pattern or simplicity, which explains why finding any pattern to the primes has proven so difficult in base-10.

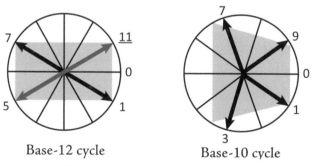

Base-12 cycle   Base-10 cycle

Geometry of the Prime Positions in Base-12 versus Base-10

To sum up, base-12 is not only more efficient and versatile than base-10 as a counting system, but also more universal as the vibrational structure of numbers themselves.

We Already Use Base-12 in Key Areas

Despite the widespread adoption of the base-10 metric system in modern society, especially in math and currency, many of our important standard measures remain in base-12 to this day. And for good reason, because they work and work well. Try to imagine how big a deal it would be change any of these long-established standards to base-10:

Time: 60 seconds in a minute and 60 minutes in a hour, 12 hours in a clock cycle, 24 hours in a day, 12 months in a year

Geometry and Trigonometry: 360 degrees in a circle, 180 degrees in a triangle, multiple of 180 degrees for a polygon

Map Coordinates: Latitude and longitude in degrees-minutes-seconds, 4 cardinal directions

Music: 12 notes or semitones in each octave of the chromatic scale

Color: 12 increments in the spectrum of the standard color wheel, where the 3 primary colors (red, yellow, blue) occur 4 positions apart, as do the 3 secondary colors (green, orange, violet), created by mixing adjacent primaries. The 6 tertiary colors are 2 positions apart, created from adjacent primary and secondary colors. Also, in each pair of the 6 complementary colors, one is opposite the other 6 positions apart.

Astrology Is in Base-12

Astrology has always been structured in base-12 with twelve signs of the zodiac and twelve houses of influence. With the recent discovery of the small planet Chiron between Saturn and Uranus, our solar system arguably also has twelve celestial bodies: the sun, the moon, Mercury, Venus, Earth, Mars, Jupiter, Saturn, Chiron, Uranus, Neptune, and Pluto. I say arguably because the astronomical community recently demoted poor Pluto from planetary status to the "dwarf planet" doghouse in 2006. Regardless, astrology has proven to be very accurate and a natural partner to numerology.

As both numerology and astrology utilize the vibrations of our birth date (and time and place of birth, in the case of astrology), these two systems are actually very similar. Both base a person's birth or "natal" chart upon the energies in effect at the moment of birth. This establishes the overall vibrational character we will carry through life and the types of experiences we will tend to attract as our life path "theme."

The main difference is that astrology approaches this by analyzing the relative positions and motions of the planets, sun, and moon, while numerology analyzes the numbers we encounter. This makes numerology much easier to learn. In fact, numerology goes a step further by also considering the vibrational character of our name: how we express ourselves.

And just as every number has a dual or polarized personality in numerology, so too does each sign in astrology. Aries is the energetic opposite of Libra, being positioned on the opposite side of the chart, as are the other five polarized pairings of Taurus and Scorpio, Gemini and Sagittarius, Cancer and Capricorn, Leo and Aquarius, and Virgo and Pisces. This opposition creates an energetic push-pull on us and, like all forms of duality encountered in our lives, simultaneously presents us with both challenge and opportunity for growth.

This then begs the question: If astrology and numerology are so similar as divination systems of our personal vibration and astrology is proven to be so accurate in its base-12 form, shouldn't numerology be structured in base-12 too?

It's Easy to Count in Base-12

To count in base-12, you actually only need one hand rather than two as with the base-10 ten-digit approach. Looking at the palm of your hand, just count the three phalanges of each of the four fingers of one hand, using the thumb as a pointer as you go.

An even better way of counting in base-12 is to simply picture the hour hand of a clock face. Not only does this give you a visual reminder that the numbers 10 and 11 are treated as single digits in base-12, but also that every full clock cycle of 12 "hours" adds a 1 to the tens position of your sum.

For example, adding 9 plus 7 gives a sum of 1x10 + 6x1 = 16 in base-10, or a full cycle of 10 plus an additional 6. In base-12, you would picture this as the hour hand of your clock first moving to 9 a.m., then moving another 7 hours past that to 4 p.m. Our sum in base-12 then would be 1x12 + 4x1 = 14, or a full "clock cycle" of 12 plus an extra 4.

Nature Prefers Base-12

As we gain ever greater understanding of how the universe works, the sciences are realizing just how fundamental base-12 is to many natural phenomena. From the patterns and proportions in plants, animals, DNA, photosynthesis, elements critical to life, subatomic particles, and even snowflakes, the number 12 and its factors of 2, 3, 4, and 6 appear to be the preferred organizational method of nature. As base-12 is more efficient and versatile than base-10 for dividing things up easily, this makes perfect sense.

Also, the conservation of energy is a universal law of nature that states that energy is neither created nor destroyed, only transformed. This means that all natural systems and processes must utilize energy in the most efficient and complete way possible. As numerology is all about the energy of numbers and understanding their natural vibrational characteristics at the simplest level, this requirement applies to numerology too. In this section, we will explore some of the many ways that nature uses base-12 to achieve that efficiency.

Natural Growth Follows Base-12

The familiar spiral shape we see so often in nature is built upon the golden ratio *phi*, a ratio of efficient growth and regeneration that is structured in base-12.

The patterns of sunflower and pine cone seeds follow this spiral, as do nautilus shells, hurricanes, and galaxies such as our own Milky Way. The numbers and spacing of petals on flowers, leaves on branches, and branches on trees follow the golden ratio as well. This not only provides the most efficient use of space in a radial way while providing stability to the plant but also minimizes how much leaves and branches block sunlight from each other.

These are all instances of how the golden ratio is expressed in nature in a circular or radial way, but it occurs just as frequently in a linear way in terms of relative lengths. This includes the relative lengths of the four bones of our fingers and length of our hand to forearm. But what exactly is the golden ratio and what does it have to do with base-12?

The golden ratio is basically the idea that each new generation of growth builds upon the one before in the most efficient way possible. In other words, the "child" always inherits the defining characteristics of its "parent" in the simplest way. And the simplest way to do that is not to recreate the wheel, but rather just make a smaller copy or fractal of the parent that retains the same ratio of parent-to-child traits from one generation to the next. Essentially, this means that each new generation equals the sum of the two before.

Now, if we were to put numbers to this idea and call the first generation 0 and the second generation 1, then over multiple generations the sequence would progress as follows:

$$0+1 = 1$$
$$1 + 1 = 2$$
$$1 + 2 = 3$$
$$2 + 3 = 5$$
$$3 + 5 = 8$$
$$5 + 8 = 13$$
$$8 + 13 = 21...$$

This series of 0, 1, 1, 2, 3, 5, 8, 13, 21, and so on is what is called the *Fibonacci series* and has the following property: the longer the sequence continues, the closer the ratio of any two successive generations gets to the value of the golden ratio, the irrational number 1.618... This golden ratio of 1.618:1 pops up everywhere in nature, and now we will explore why.

The most efficient way to express the golden ratio in two-dimensional physical terms is with the simplest two-dimensional shape, the triangle, so this is what nature uses to put it into practice. Not just any triangle will do, but a *golden triangle* with the base-12 angles of 36, 72, and 72 degrees. This is because it is the only triangle whose longer and shorter sides are in golden ratio proportion.

This enables a smaller "child" triangle to be created from the "parent" triangle such that the long side of the "parent" becomes the short side of the "child," thus preserving the golden ratio shape for the next generation and beyond. This process can be continued indefinitely, creating an infinite number of golden triangles. The logarithmic "golden spiral" is the shape this creates if an outer curve is then drawn connecting the end points of all the long "inherited" sides of the nested triangles. This is the trademark spiral shape of nature, all courtesy of base-12.

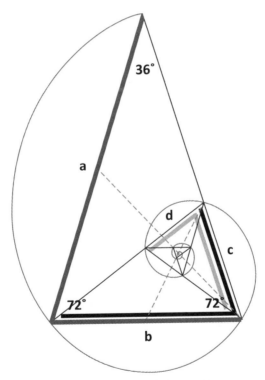

**Logarithmic Spiral Consisting
of Nested Golden Triangles**

The Basic Ingredients for Life Are Base-12

Carbon composes 12 percent of the atoms in the human body and is critical to all life on Earth. So too is oxygen, which makes up another 24 percent. Only hydrogen plays a bigger role at 62 percent. Together, these three elements account for 98 percent of all the atoms of you and me. These three fundamental elements along with sunlight, liquid water, and photosynthesis are arguably the most important prerequisites for life and, as we will see, are all structured in base-12.

Sunlight

Let's start with sunlight. Without the light and warmth provided by the sun and in just the right amount, Earth would not be able to support life nor the liquid water and oxygen (through photosynthesis) upon which life depends. This brings us to the process within each star that makes its own helium as fuel to keep the lights burning brightly. Actually, there's a couple of different processes depending on the size of the star.

For stars about the size of our sun and smaller, four hydrogen atoms are converted into helium through a three-step fusion process called the proton-proton chain reaction. For stars about 1.3 times the size of our sun and larger, the main helium-forming process at work instead is the carbon-nitrogen-oxygen cycle, or CNO cycle for short. This process converts four hydrogen atoms into helium through a six-step fusion cycle that uses carbon-12 as the catalyst. Both of these methods of producing helium rely on various base-12 combinations of 3, 4, 6, and 12.

Also, once a star has produced enough helium, another fusion process kicks in, called the triple-alpha process, which then converts three helium nuclei (also called "alpha particles") into a carbon-12 nucleus. Eventually, the process begins to convert carbon-12 into oxygen and other heavier elements. This is where all the carbon-12 and oxygen initially came from that made us possible.

Carbon

Perhaps the ultimate base-12 element is carbon. The carbon atom has six positively charged protons and six negatively charged electrons for a total of twelve, making it neutral overall. Of the stable isotopes of carbon that exist on Earth, carbon-12, which is denoted ^{12}C, is by far the most abundant at nearly 99 percent. This, again, is because carbon-12 is the primary type of carbon produced by stars, as discussed earlier. An isotope is a version of the same basic element that has a different number of neutrons, which are neutral in charge.

In the carbon-12 atom, there are 6 neutrons in addition to the six protons and six electrons of the base carbon atom. Carbon-12 is very stable, not decaying into other forms or elements over time, and is particularly versatile. In fact, it is the most versatile of all known elements, capable of a huge range of properties, from the softness, opacity, and electrical conductivity of graphite to the extreme hardness, transparency, and resistivity of diamond.

Carbon's impressive creative range likewise extends to the vast number of compounds it's able to form with other elements, again more than any other element. This is due to carbon being the smallest atom with four outer electrons, making it very easy to combine with other atoms in many diverse ways. Note how this precisely mirrors the base-12 cycle itself, where four prime number positions can generate every other possible integer. In short, the highly base-12 structure of carbon and carbon-12 gives this element the same superior flexibility of the base-12 number system, so much so that all known physical lifeforms on Earth are carbon-based.

Oxygen

The oxygen atom consists of eight protons and eight electrons. The stable isotope form that is most abundant at over 99 percent is oxygen-16, ^{16}O, which includes the addition of eight neutrons. Since oxygen is highly reactive, it likes to join in pairs to form the stable oxygen molecule O_2. Like carbon-12, the oxygen molecule ends up with four outer electrons on each of the two atoms once joined. This makes oxygen very receptive to combining with many other elements and compounds, once again mirroring the four prime positions of the base-12 cycle.

Water

Next, we have the water molecule H_2O, which makes up approximately 60 percent of our bodies by weight and is crucial for cells to function, digestion to work, and body temperature to remain in control. The neutral water molecule consists of two hydrogen atoms bonded to one oxygen atom. This creates the V-shaped structure that, like the carbon-12 atom, is very compact in size and features four free electrons to combine easily with other things.

Not only does this once again impart the versatility of the base-12 prime pattern, but it even resembles its shape and structure. This includes the water molecule having an inherent polarity due to that shape, with the top half of the molecule slightly positive in charge and the lower half slightly negative. This enables water molecules to attract each other easily despite each molecule being neutral overall—the same polarized nature of numerology, in which every number vibration has a range of both positive and negative traits while the overall cycle achieves neutrality, always returning to the 0 of potential.

Of course, we can't very well discuss the base-12 nature of water without honorable mention of snowflakes. Snowflakes are ice crystals that form in the atmosphere under sufficiently cold and moist conditions. They typically contain 6 sides or branches due to the V-shaped structure of the water molecule wanting to join other water molecules in a hexagonal or six-sided pattern. This hexagonal growth pattern continues as the snowflake falls through the changing conditions of its descent, accounting for the infinite variety of final snowflake patterns possible. Occasionally snowflakes take on other shapes, such as three-sided or twelve-sided, but these are relatively rare. They never, however, take on a five-sided or ten-sided (i.e., base-10) form.

Photosynthesis

Now that we have light, carbon, oxygen, and liquid water, we have everything we need to continuously regenerate the oxygen we breathe through photosynthesis. Photosynthesis is the chemical process by which plants and algae use sunlight to convert carbon dioxide and water into glucose as food and oxygen as a waste product. Thus, the carbon dioxide that humans and all other animals exhale as waste keeps alive the algae and plants that generate oxygen as waste, which keeps us alive.

In true base-12 fashion, photosynthesis transforms six molecules each of carbon dioxide and water into six of oxygen, along with glucose. Even the glucose molecule is highly base-12 with twelve hydrogen atoms joined to six carbon and six oxygen.

DNA Follows the Base-12 Pattern

The double-spiral waveform of the base-12 numerology blueprint is remarkably similar to the structure of the double helix spiral of the DNA molecule, right down to the constant spacing between the two spirals and the asymmetrical offset at the center of each wavelength. Both are remarkably similar in function too.

Just as DNA contains the entire blueprint for making a complete living organism from only four bases (adenine, thymine, guanine, and cytosine), the base-12 prime pattern contains the entire blueprint to describe any set of number frequencies from only four prime positions (1, 5, 7 and 11). In this way, both provide a geometric recipe for creating complex diversity from the fewest building blocks, all made possible by base-12. Even the size of the DNA molecule itself is in the golden ratio proportion of 34 angstroms long by 21 angstroms wide for each full cycle of its double helix spiral.

The Subatomic World Is Base-12

The Standard Model of particle physics is our current understanding of the smallest known building blocks of matter and follows base-12 and its factors of 2, 3, 4, and 6 precisely.

In this model, there are twelve elementary matter particles called fermions and four force carriers called gauge bosons. The twelve fermions consist of six quarks (three with a +2/3 charge and three with a −1/3 charge) and six leptons (three with a −1 charge and three that are neutral with 0 charge). These are further grouped into three "generations" of four based on related properties. Even the way the six quarks combine together follows a "three-color" rule. Of those twelve fermions, only three are used to create all physical matter: the up quark, the down quark, and the electron. Together, they combine in various ways to form the atoms of every known element in the periodic table.

The four types of gauge bosons are the photon, gluon, W, and Z. Last, there's the Higgs boson, which is the particle expression of the Higgs field that interacts with all the other particles to give them their masses. This makes the Higgs boson the "big shot" that carries a lot of weight in the base-12 subatomic world, literally.

Of all the examples we have just covered of the base-12 bias of nature, the structure of the subatomic world is perhaps our strongest evidence that base-12 *is* the underlying number system of nature. After all, everything in the physical universe is built from the subatomic particles and their forces—atoms, molecules, plants, animals, planets, stars, and galaxies. So it makes sense that if the smallest building blocks of matter are structured in base-12, then everything made from them should follow the same pattern.

The next logical question then is why the subatomic world follows base-12 in the first place. I believe this is where the base-12 prime vibration itself comes in, the same vibrational blueprint of base-12 numerology. Since the Higgs field is what orchestrates all the subatomic particles and forces into their base-12 structure, I suspect the Higgs field and base-12 prime vibration are one and the same. But that's for another book!

Numerology Readings Are More Accurate in Base-12

Last but not least, I use base-12 for numerology because it consistently provides more accurate readings than base-10. Here we will take a look at a couple of famous people that most readers will know, Nikola Tesla and Lady Diana, and compare their main numbers using both approaches.

Don't worry about how the numbers were calculated and defined for now—it will all make sense later. Just follow along and you will get an idea of the power of base-12 in action.

Nikola Tesla, Born July 10, 1856

Nikola Tesla was a brilliant engineer, prolific inventor, and designer of the alternating current electrical system.

	Base-10	Base-12
Life Path (birth date):	10/1	21/3
Expression (birth name):	11	23/5
Maturity (Life Path + Expression):	12/3	8
Soul (vowels in name):	13/4	<u>11</u>
Personality (consonants):	7	14/5
Karmic Lessons (missing letters):	4, 7, 8	4, 7, 8

Life Path: Why You Are Here,
Main Theme to Explore, and Lessons to Learn

Tesla's life path in base-10 is the 10/1 of new beginnings, self, and independence (1) through new beginnings (1) of potential (0), and in base-12 it is the 21/3 of the catalyst (3) through the duality (2) of new beginnings and independence (1).

On the surface, his life's work was certainly about turning promising ideas into practical inventions and doing so in a very solitary way (1) as per his base-10 life path. However, his broader impact as revealed by his base-12 number was as a catalyst (3) for technological advancement by harnessing the duality (2) of his life and his independent nature (1).

Not only did his work with such things as AC electricity, radio, and opposed magnetic fields explore duality from a technical perspective, his business dealings and personal life were very polarized as well. Most notably, he had a very public rivalry with Thomas Edison and his competing technology of DC electricity.

Even their personalities were a study in duality: Edison the business-savvy capitalist and Tesla the innocent idealist.

His last business venture involving wireless energy transmission was also fraught with hardship to the point of bankruptcy and Tesla died a poor recluse at the age of 86. Still, even the timing of his passing has deep significance in base-12, as 86 converts to the 72/9 of completion (9) through spiritual truth and knowledge (7) of duality (2). A fitting acknowledgement that he completed what he set out to do for his life path, which was to learn about duality in a comprehensive way. In base-10, on the other hand, 86 reduces to the 14/5 of change (5) through new beginnings (1) of structure and stability (4). This would suggest a more general interpretation of his life's work as creating change (5) through innovative (1) technology (4).

Expression Number: Who You Are and How You Can Best Express Yourself

Tesla's expression number in base-10 is the 11 master number of illumination and in base-12 the 23/5 of change (5) through the duality (2) of catalysts (3).

Here, base-10 describes the man as an inspirational visionary and innovator, which is certainly true. However, at a more fundamental level, as revealed in base-12, he was a restless agent of change (5) who used duality (2) as a catalyst (3) for driving that change. He faced duality and conflict in all areas of his work and personal life, but this seemed to galvanize his resolve rather than defeat him.

Where his 21/3 life path enabled him to learn about the catalyst theme through the tough teacher of duality, his 23/5 expression number gave him the disposition and talent to use that duality constructively as a catalyst for technological advancement. As such, base-12 provides a more comprehensive picture of who Tesla was.

Maturity Number: Focus for the Later Part of Your Life (After 35)

In base-10, Tesla's maturity number is the 12/3 of the catalyst (3) through new beginnings (1) of duality (2) and in base-12 it is the 8 of manifestation and abundance.

I would say that both base-10 and base-12 numbers are accurate assessments of his later adult years, but the base-12 result is the more fundamental theme being explored.

Consistent with the 12/3 result of base-10, he faced increasing (1) opposition and lack of support for his ideas (2), and this was the catalyst (3) for his eventual financial demise. On a more basic level, the base-12 result of 8 indicates how his later years were all about exploring the theme of abundance and lack (8). This included many unsuccessful attempts at manifesting his increasingly ambitious projects or even manifesting a livelihood for himself. Regardless, in both approaches we see how this stage of his life was focused on exploring the negative side of his maturity number theme.

It's also interesting to note that the final stage of his life path, called the third growth cycle and based upon his year of birth, is the 2 of duality in base-10 and the 8 of manifestation in base-12. Whenever a person's third growth cycle matches their maturity number, they will experience that theme directly and intensely as the last major lesson of their life. This is the case in base-12, where both are the 8 theme, whereas base-10 suggests a more indirect connection between a 3 maturity number and 2 growth cycle. Based on how extreme Tesla's manifestation challenges were later in life, this adds further validation to the base-12 approach.

Soul Number: Inner Yearning and What Most Fulfills You

Tesla's soul number in base-10 is the 13/4 of structure and stability (4) through new beginnings (1) of the catalyst (3) versus the 11 of illumination in base-12.

The base-12 result is far more accurate here than the base-10. Everything we know about Tesla indicates he was anything but the conservative, cautious, and risk-averse 4 type. His amazing personal accomplishments and the drive, passion, and vision that fueled them all validate an inner yearning for illumination and discovery as indicated in base-12.

Another way to compare the accuracy of base-12 versus base-10 is to see how well the yearning of his soul number supports the mission of his life path. In base-12, his life path is the 3 of the catalyst and soul number the 11 of illumination. This would suggest that his greatest goal was to be a catalyst of illumination for others more so than himself. This sounds very accurate with the enormous technological impact he had globally though at great personal cost and sacrifice. In base-10 on the other hand, his life path is the 1 of new beginnings and independence and his soul number the 4 of structure and stability. This instead suggests that his greatest goal was to create structure and stability for himself, which is far from the truth.

Personality Number: Outer Personality and How Others See You

Last, Tesla's personality number according to base-10 is the 7 of spiritual truth and knowledge versus the 14/5 of change (5) through new beginnings (1) of structure and stability (4) in base-12.

Although Tesla was a spiritual person and raised by a father who was an Orthodox priest, he wasn't outwardly spiritual nor did he follow any particular religion during his adult life. His personality was, however, most definitely of a highly intelligent person who spoke eloquently on many topics. In this regard, his personality matched the base-10 result somewhat. Still, the base-12 portrayal of Tesla is even more accurate as a restless and daring pioneer (5) who was original, independent, and driven (1) but highly organized, disciplined, and practical (4).

Karmic Lessons: Unfinished Lessons from
Prior Lives and Weaknesses to Resolve

When the letters of his birth name *Nikola Tesla* are converted to numbers, we get 592631 25131. We see that Tesla's karmic lessons, number energies missing from his name, include the 4 of structure and stability, the 7 of spiritual truth and knowledge, and the 8 of abundance and manifestation.

As karmic lessons, these are the vibrational "gaps" he placed in his name to serve as weaknesses he would need to work hard to resolve. Consequently, these would play out as his toughest obstacles in life, which indeed they were—achieving personal and financial stability (4), finding spiritual truth (7), and manifesting abundance (8). This makes sense for how we have characterized Nikola Tesla's life here, particularly from the base-12 approach.

Diana Frances Spencer, Born July 1, 1961

Diana Frances Spencer was Princess of Wales, a humanitarian, and an advocate for many charitable causes, including children's hospitals, AIDS awareness, and the banning of landmines.

	Base-10	Base-12
Life Path (birth date):	16/7	11
Expression (birth name):	13/4	26/8
Maturity (Life Path + Expression):	11	17/8
Soul (vowels in name):	18/9	23/5
Personality (consonants):	26/8	16/7
Karmic Lessons (missing letters):	2, 8	2, 8

Life Path: Why You Are Here,
Main Theme to Explore, and Lessons to Learn

Diana's life path in base-10 is the 16/7 of spiritual truth and knowledge (7) through new beginnings (1) of love and harmony (6), and in base-12 it is the 11 of illumination.

It's fair to say that Diana did seek a spiritually and emotionally fulfilling life (7) as indicated in base-10, particularly in her personal quest (1) for finding and sharing love (6). However, the higher purpose of her life path was clearly to illuminate truth (11). Not only did she shed light on the many humanitarian causes she supported but also on the issue of privacy, being under the relentless spot light of the media. Her personal life, including her troubled marriage and romantic relationships, were on constant public display.

Having an <u>11</u> life path also meant that she was prone to the <u>11</u>'s lower tendencies of being very independent, defiant, disillusioned, and depressed when feeling disempowered.

Diana died on August 31, 1997, in a car crash in a Paris tunnel while reportedly being pursued by paparazzi. This date reduces to 2 in base-10 or <u>11</u>1/10/1 in base-12. Beyond the sadness and public outcry represented by the polarized 2 of base-10, her death was a singular global event (1) of profound illumination (<u>11</u>) as revealed in base-12. This in turn marked a new beginning (1) of potential (0) for media ethics and a new beginning (1) for Diana's own ongoing spiritual journey. Even her passing in a tunnel was symbolic of her life's theme of navigating through darkness in order to reach light.

Expression Number: Who You Are
and How You Can Best Express Yourself

Diana's expression number in base-10 is the 13/4 of structure and stability (4) through new beginnings (1) of the catalyst (3) and in base-12 the 26/8 of manifestation and abundance (8) through the duality (2) of love and harmony (6).

Although she was definitely reserved and responsible and sought stability (4), as suggested by base-10, her deeper calling and strength was to persevere in manifesting something good (8) out of conflicted situations (2) lacking love and harmony (6), per base-12.

She demonstrated this in all areas of her life; she endured a fragmented childhood with the divorce of her parents when she was seven, she followed her heart in the search of happiness despite her conflicted marriage, she was drawn to polarized causes where she felt she could make a difference and she dealt with her own polarized battle with public popularity and low self-esteem. Her 26/8 theme of abundance through the duality of love was perhaps most powerfully expressed through her two boys, William and Harry, the true loves of her life.

Maturity Number: Focus for the Later Part of Your Life (After 35)

Diana's maturity number is the <u>11</u> of illumination in base-10 versus the 17/8 of manifestation and abundance (8) through new beginnings (1) of spiritual truth and knowledge (7) in base-12. Again, the maturity number indicates one's main focus for the second half of their life, after age thirty-five.

As Diana passed at age 36, her passing itself was how she expressed her maturity number theme. It was both a moment of illumination for all of us as per base-10 and a new beginning of spiritual truth for herself as per base-12. However, the base-12 maturity number theme of 17/8 makes particular sense relative to her 26/8 expression number, as both seek to manifest abundance (8), only in different ways. In life, she championed the cause for creating good (8) from situations lacking (2) love (6), while in death she achieved that abundance through a spiritual new beginning (17). Even Diana's informal title as the "people's princess" resonates with the 1 + 7 = 8 vibration of her maturity number in base-12.

Soul Number: Inner Yearning and What Most Fulfills You

Diana's soul number in base-10 is the 18/9 of completion (9) through new beginnings (1) of manifestation (8) and in base-12 the 23/5 of change (5) through the duality (2) of catalysts (3).

Here I think base-10 reflects her yearning for a sense of accomplishment and making a difference, whereas base-12 explains in greater depth how she wished to accomplish that:

She sought change (5) for a better world through the many charities she served and change for a better life for herself. She did this on the public front by taking on challenging issues (2) such as landmines, AIDS, cancer, and mental illness. In her personal life, she experienced both sides of the "change" theme through the many catalytic circumstances (3) she found herself in and her many efforts to cope. On the positive side, she used her public profile and influence as a catalyst for positive change in her humanitarian efforts, while on the negative side, she felt quite powerless in her highly scrutinized role as a member of the royal family.

From a higher perspective, Diana clearly yearned to explore the theme of change (5) from both extremes (2) of the catalytic spectrum (3) as both powerful catalyst and disempowered victim of circumstance. This matches her base-12 soul number of 23/5 perfectly.

Personality Number: Outer Personality and How Others See You

Last, Diana's personality number according to base-10 is the 26/8 of manifestation and abundance (8) through duality (2) of love and harmony (6) versus the 16/7 of spiritual truth (7) through new beginnings (1) of love and harmony (6) in base-12.

A person with an 8 personality number is typically practical and grounded with a lot of business savvy, none of which really describes Diana's persona. However, the base-12 result of 16/7 seems spot on. She most definitely gave the impression of a spiritually deep and empathic person (7) and one who took the initiative (1) to make others feel appreciated and loved (6).

Also, the 16 of base-12 reflects the hopeful and optimistic person that Diana was: one who didn't give up on finding love but rather continued searching through many new beginnings. The 26 of base-10 portrays instead a pessimistic person unlike Diana, one jaded and defeated in love and cautious of the "duality" in others.

Karmic Lessons: Unfinished Lessons from Prior Lives and Weaknesses to Resolve

When the letters of her birth name *Diana Frances Spencer* are converted to numbers, we obtain 49151 6915351 1755359. We see that Diana's karmic lessons, the number energies missing from her name, include the 2 of duality and the 8 of manifestation and abundance.

These karmic lessons are the vibrational weaknesses she built into her name in order to dig deeply into those themes. She therefore sought many experiences that tested her ability to deal with duality (2) and to overcome obstacles in manifesting abundance (8). As her base-12 expression number of 26/8 features those same themes, we see that she intentionally set herself on a direct course with her two greatest weaknesses. This is a sign of a courageous soul who took on a very challenging life in order to accelerate her spiritual growth.

2

WHAT IS
BASE-12 NUMEROLOGY?

Now that we have an appreciation of the merits of base-12, let's see how it ties in to numerology. In this chapter, we cover what numerology is and how it began and compare the traditional base-10 approach with the base-12 method we will be exploring in this book.

We will review the two basic steps involved in determining the numerology of any number, which is to first convert the number from base-10 to base-12 and then "reduce" it to a single-digit. This final single-digit number reveals the vibrational personality of the original number.

Next, we explain how to determine the base-12 numerology of any word. We see how words are handled the same way as numbers, except for an extra preliminary step of converting the individual letters in the word to numbers. We also learn what inner and outer energies are and how they give deeper meaning to any number you obtain when doing numerology. Examples are given for everything we cover here, as well as handy base-10 to base-12 conversion tables for any number you're likely to come across.

We wrap up the chapter with an overview of a variety of popular applications for numerology, from the personal numerology reading, which will be our focus, to changing your name, naming a baby, selecting a name for a business or website, or choosing an address. We will also show how you can use regular playing cards as a numerology oracle deck for gaining insight into any question you may have.

The Origins of Numerology

Every number has a dual personality: its normal face value that we use to count and calculate in our daily activities and its less understood energetic quality. Words and letters likewise have a vibrational character beyond their surface meaning. It is this vibrational quality of numbers and letters and how they resonate (or clash) with our own vibration in predictable ways that is the basis of numerology. In this way, numerology reveals the energetic character of a name, date, place, or anything that can be expressed in numbers or letters.

There are various forms of numerology, but the one most widely used today is the Pythagorean or "Western" system developed over 2,500 years ago by the Greek mathematician Pythagoras. To determine the vibrational quality of any number or word using this system, we add together the numbers or number values of letters using the table below.

1	2	3	4	5	6	7	8	9
A	B	C	D	E	F	G	H	I
J	K	L	M	N	O	P	Q	R
S	T	U	V	W	X	Y	Z	

Table 1. Pythagorean Number-Letter Table

We then "reduce" the resulting total to a single digit by adding those numbers together, except for master numbers like 11, 22, or 33 (more on that later). Last, we interpret the result using established meanings. That's the basics of numerology in a nutshell.

Note that the Pythagorean system of numerology uses the decimal system, also known as base-10, with its energy cycle including the numbers from 0 to 9. This is the normal method of counting we use today. I first began my study of numerology using base-10 as that quite frankly was all that was available to study. Although various number base systems were adopted over the ages, it was base-10 that was in use at the time of Pythagoras in Greece and by the earlier Chaldeans for their numerological systems.

In the case of Chaldean numerology, the number 9 was excluded from the number table as it was considered sacred. They also assigned letters to numbers according to what they believed each letter's vibration to be, rather than the Pythagorean approach of position in the alphabet.

Base-12 Numerology versus Traditional Base-10

The difference between base-12 and base-10 is to count in cycles of 12 (i.e., from 0 to 11) instead of cycles of 10 (i.e., from 0 to 9). As such, the numbers 10 and 11 in base-12 are treated as single digits with distinct energies, just like the numbers 1 through 9. Also, 0 represents the completion of one cycle and the potential of the next, the same role that 0 plays in base-10.

As mentioned in the introduction, the 10 and 11 are underlined whenever they occur as single digits (i.e., within the first cycle of base-12) to tell them apart from double-digit 10s and 11s. This is important as the single digit 10 and 11 are not to be reduced further when they appear in sums of numbers, whereas the double digit 10 and 11 are to be reduced.

Another clarification I should make is that I still use the original Pythagorean number-letter table to determine the 1 to 9 number vibration of individual letters, rather than the Chaldean method or some other alternative. The only difference is that I then convert any sum I get to base-12 before reducing it to determine the combined vibration of a word. My reasoning for staying with the Pythagorean system is as follows.

First, the Pythagorean approach of assigning letters to the same number vibration as their position in the alphabet seems logical to me. The alphabet itself is a cycle after all with a specific sequence. Just as the order of the numbers has a progressive meaning from lower to higher, so too does the sequence of letters in the alphabet.

This is not to say that the Chaldean method was incorrect by any means, just different. Same goes for every other version of numerology, such as the Mayan, Vedic, and Chinese. I believe that each system of numerology was accurate for the civilization that followed it because each society adopted an interpretation that resonated with their culture at the time and that they followed consistently. The Pythagorean method simply appeals to me personally as it is the most current and the one that follows our modern alphabet and the numerical order or "energetic intent" we give to that alphabet.

Second, I feel attempting to regroup the twenty-six letters of the alphabet from rows of nine into rows of eleven would scramble their original meaning and the letter vibrations assigned. I believe that ancient societies such as the Greeks had a closer connection with nature and a clearer intuition and sensitivity regarding energy than does modern society today and that their time-honored interpretations are accurate.

Last, the single-digit numbers of 10 and 11 in base-12, though vibrating with their own distinct energies, are also *relationship energies* consistent with base-10. What I mean is that both the 10 and 11 reflect different aspects of the 1 and 0 energies in relationship to each other. The 10, for instance, represents an energy of awareness, of the 1 of the individual self seeing the 0 of potential and connectedness. Likewise, the 11 denotes the energy of illumination, of the 1 of self seeing its true nature reflected in experiences it encounters. As the 1 and 0 have the same meanings in base-10 and base-12, the 10 and 11 are still derived from the base-10 number energies of 1 and 0, which further supports the use of the Pythagorean base-10 number-letter chart.

In short, I feel that retaining the original letter assignments of the Pythagorean system coupled with nature's cycle of base-12 offers the best of both worlds.

That said, I believe all forms of numerology can provide great insight into the energy of our human experience, provided the practitioner is consistent and disciplined in their approach. So, with that bit of background under our belts, let's get working with the numbers.

Converting Numbers to Base-12 and Reducing to Single Digits

Our first step is to get comfortable with converting a base-10 number into its base-12 equivalent and then reducing that number into a single digit. That's the only math you will need to become a certifiable numerology whiz.

When you work with any number base system, you need to follow that base's cycle when performing arithmetic with those numbers. Again, base-10 works in the familiar cycles of 10 and base-12 in "clock" cycles of 12.

Returning to our earlier example of picturing base-12 as clock cycles in the section "It's Easy to Count in Base-12" on page 12, let's say we were adding together the numbers 9 and 7 in base-10. We would get a total of 16, which then reduces to $1 + 6 = 7$ to give us a final single digit. This is because we treat each "cycle" of 10 as a completed lap of one 10, so $9 + 7$ would equal one cycle of 10 plus 6 left over as a remainder. Likewise, in base-12, $9 + 7$ would equal one cycle of 12 plus another 4 as a remainder, or $1 \times 12 + 4 = 14$, which further reduces to $1 + 4 = 5$ as the final single digit.

This "taking the remainder" approach, by the way, is what is called modular arithmetic in traditional mathematics, so it's nothing mysterious. As the remainder is the unique portion of a number that remains after the common divisor or "modulus" is removed, that remainder is the unique vibration that numerology isolates. As such, I'm confident that an expanded application of modular arithmetic will help resolve many open problems in mathematics and physics and eventually convince the scientific community of the validity of numerology once and for all.

Larger numbers, such as my year of birth of 1963, are a little trickier to convert from base-10 to base-12 and reduce but easy once you get the hang of it. Let's walk through the process for both base-10 and base-12 to get a feel for it.

Example: Reducing 1963 to a Single Digit in Base-10

In base-10, we're familiar with how 1963 consists of $1 \times 1,000 + 9 \times 100 + 6 \times 10 +$ remainder of 3. This is equivalent to $1 \times 10^3 + 9 \times 10^2 + 6 \times 10^1 + 3 \times 10^0$. We're basically breaking the number down into its various powers of 10, starting with the largest multiple of 10 that can fit within the number, as shown in the following table.

1,000s (10^3)	**100s** (10^2)	**10s** (10^1)	**1s** (10^0)	
1 x 1,000	-	-	-	=**1,000**
	9 x 100	-	-	=**900**
		6 x 10	-	=**60**
			3 x 1	=**3**
			Sum	=**1,963**

Table 2. The Year 1963 in Base-10

As 1,000 divides into 1,963 only once, the thousands column becomes 1x1,000 = 1,000 with a remainder of 963. As 100 fits into 963 nine times, the hundreds column becomes 9 x 100 = 900 with a remainder of 63. Next, 10 fits into 63 six times so the tens column becomes 6 x 10 = 60 with a final remainder of 3.

In base-10 numerology, reducing 1963 to its final single digit involves first adding all four of its digits together, which gives 1 + 9 + 6 + 3 = 19. As 19 is not yet a single digit, we repeat the process by adding the two digits of 19 together, which gives 1 + 9 = 10. As 10 still isn't a single digit number in base-10, we need to repeat the process once more by adding the two digits of 10 together, which gives our final single digit result of 1 + 0 = 1. Step by step, it looks like the following:

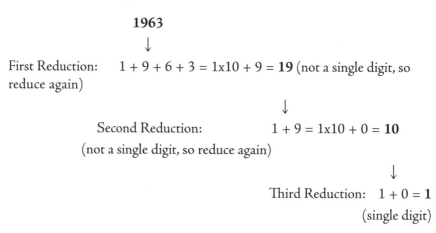

1963

↓

First Reduction: 1 + 9 + 6 + 3 = 1x10 + 9 = **19** (not a single digit, so reduce again)

↓

Second Reduction: 1 + 9 = 1x10 + 0 = **10**
(not a single digit, so reduce again)

↓

Third Reduction: 1 + 0 = **1**
(single digit)

Table 3. Reducing the Year 1963 to a Single Digit in Base-10

Example: Converting 1963 to Base-12
before Reducing to a Single Digit

It works the very same way in base-12 numerology, except we use powers of 12 instead of 10. So, in base-12, the largest power of 12 that can divide into 1963 is 12^3 or 1728. As 1,728 divides into 1,963 only once with a remainder of 235, our thousands column becomes 1 x 1,000 = 1,000. As 12^2 or 144 fits into 235 only once with a remainder of 91, the hundreds column becomes 1 x 100 = 100. Next, as 12^1 or 12 fits into 91 seven times or 84 with a remainder of 7, the tens column becomes 7x10 = 70 with a final remainder of 7. Putting this all together, 1963 in base-10 equals $1x12^3 + 1x12^2 + 7x12 + 7$ or 1,177 in base-12, summarized in the table below.

1,000s (12^3)	**100s** (12^2)	**10s** (12^1)	**1s** (12^0)	
1 x 1,728	-	-	-	= 1,000
	1 x 144	-	-	= 100
		7 x 12		= 70
			7 x 1	= 7
			Sum	= **1,177**

Table 4. Converting 1963 from Base-10 to Base-12

As in base-10 numerology, the first step in reducing 1,177 to a single digit in base-12 involves adding all four of its digits together. However, now that we're thinking in cycles of 12s instead of 10s, our sum becomes 1 + 1 + 7 + 7 = 1x12 + 4 = 14. As 14 is not yet a single digit in base-12, we repeat the process by adding the two digits of 14 together, which gives our final single digit result of 1 + 4 = 5. Step by step, this looks like the following:

1,177
↓
First Reduction: 1+1+7+7 = 1x12+4 = **14** (not a single digit, so reduce again)
↓
Second Reduction: 1+4 = **5** (single digit)

As you can see, converting base-10 numbers to base-12 isn't too painful. Still, I appreciate it takes some getting used to after a lifetime of thinking in terms of tens. Not to worry though: every number you may come across while doing your own numerology chart is already converted and reduced for you in the following two tables.

The first table, "Base-10 to Base-12 Conversions from 1 to 100," gives the base-12 equivalent for any day, month, or name you will likely encounter, and the second table, "Base-10 to Base-12 Conversions for Year Starting in 1915," provides the base-12 numbers for any birth year. Bookmark these pages, as you will refer to them often.

Base 10	Base-12 reduced	Base 10	Base-12 reduced	Base 10	Base-12 reduced	Base 10	Base-12 reduced
1 (Jan)	1	26	22	51	43/7	76	64/10
2 (Feb)	2	27	23/5	52	44	77	65/11
3 (Mar)	3	28	24/6	53	45/9	78	66
4 (Apr)	4	29	25/7	54	46/10	79	67/11
5 (May)	5	30	26/8	55	47/11	80	68/12/3
6 (Jun)	6	31	27/9	56	48/10/1	81	69/13/4
7 (Jul)	7	32	28/10	57	49/11	82	610/14/5
8 (Aug)	8	33	29/11	58	410/12/3	83	611/15/6
9 (Sep)	9	34	210/10/1	59	411/13/4	84	70/7
10 (Oct)	10	35	211/11	60	50/5	85	71/8
11 (Nov)	11	36	30/3	61	51/6	86	72/9
12 (Dec)	10/1	37	31/4	62	52/7	87	73/10
13	11	38	32/5	63	53/8	88	74/11
14	12/3	39	33	64	54/9	89	75/10/1
15	13/4	40	34/7	65	55	90	76/11
16	14/5	41	35/8	66	56/11	91	77
17	15/6	42	36/9	67	57/10/1	92	78/13/4
18	16/7	43	37/10	68	58/11	93	79/14/5
19	17/8	44	38/11	69	59/12/3	94	710/15/6
20	18/9	45	39/10/1	70	510/13/4	95	711/16/7
21	19/10	46	310/11	71	511/14/5	96	80/8
22	110/11	47	311/12/3	72	60/6	97	81/9
23	111/10/1	48	40/4	73	61/7	98	82/10
24	20/2	49	41/5	74	62/8	99	83/11
25	21/3	50	42/6	75	63/9	100	84/10/1

Table 5. Base-10 to Base-12 Conversions from 1 to 100
*Master numbers shown in bold italic.

YEAR (in Base-10)										Base-12 reduced
1915	1926	1937	1948	1959	1970	1981	1992	2003	2014	10/1
									2015	20/2
1916	1927	1938	1949	1960	1971	1982	1993	2004		*11*
									2016	**3**
1917	1928	1939	1950	1961	1972	1983	1994	2005		12/3
									2017	**4**
1918	1929	1940	1951	1962	1973	1984	1995	2006		13/4
									2018	**5**
1919	1930	1941	1952	1963	1974	1985	1996	2007		14/5
1920									2019	**6**
	1931	1942	1953	1964	1975	1986	1997	2008		15/6
1921	1932								2020	**7**
		1943	1954	1965	1976	1987	1998	2009		16/7
1922	1933	1944							2021	**8**
			1955	1966	1977	1988	1999	2010		17/8
1923	1934	1945	1956						2022	**9**
				1967	1978	1989	2000	2011		18/9
1924	1935	1946	1957	1968					2023	**10**
					1979	1990	2001	2012		19/**10**
1925	1936	1947	1958	1969	1980				2024	**11**
						1991	2002	2013		1**10**/**11**

Table 6. Base-10 to Base-12 Conversions for Year Starting in 1915

The Numerology of Words

Let's now use the words *nature* and *business* to see how we convert words to their energetic values.

For the word *nature*, we first look up the number corresponding to N on our Pythagorean number-letter table (see page 30), which is 5. We then add to it the number corresponding to every other letter. This gives us a total of 25 in base-10, which is equivalent to $2 \times 12 + 1 = 21$ in base-12.

However, we aren't done yet, as we need to keep reducing until we end up with a single digit (unless we have a master number such as 11, 22, or 33 that doesn't get reduced further, more on that later). So, we add the 2 and the 1 together to get our single-digit energy of 3. The final reduced digit (3) reflects the *outer energy* being projected, while the two individual digits that added together to give that number (2 + 1) reveal the *inner influences*.

Nature: 5 + 1 + 2 + 3 + 9 + 5 = 25 in base-10 = 2x12 + 1 = 21 in base-12 = 2 + 1 = 3 or 21/3

Business: 2 + 3 + 1 + 9 + 5 + 5 + 1 + 1 = 27 in base-10 = 2x12 + 3 = 23 in base-12 = 2 + 3 = 5 or 23/5

The notation typically used by numerologists for this would be 21/3, where the outer energy of the 3 is being expressed through the inner energies of the 2 and the 1. Following the same method for *business*, we get a base-12 number energy of 2 + 3 = 5 or 23/5, where the 5 energy is expressed through the 2 and the 3.

Inner and Outer Energies

A helpful way to think of this idea of "inner" and "outer" energies is in terms of music. Every single-digit number is like a single note being played with a unique sound and vibrational frequency all its own. When played together with other notes, it can create a chord if played at the same time or a melody if played individually.

Number energies, like music, also possess multiple levels of meaning depending upon their relationship to other numbers. So, to get the full value out of numerology, it's important to consider both the individual numbers before reduction and the reduced number they combine to produce.

Note that you won't always get a two-digit number before your final reduction, such as with the word *cat*, since C + A + T = 3 + 1 + 2 = 6. Here, you get to a single digit right away without having to reduce further. This simply means that the 6 energy is expressed *directly* by this word, not *indirectly* through two other numbers as inner influences.

The Personal Numerology Reading

The main application of numerology today, and the focus of this book, is for personal numerology readings. Although the format of readings can vary widely from one numerologist to the next, the content is generally the same and based on two numbers: your birth date and your full birth name. Sometimes readings will also include an analysis of other supplementary personal information, such as a person's current name (the name they prefer to use on a daily basis) and specific dates or years of interest. However, the birth date and birth name are the foundation of every reading for the following reason.

Your birth date and birth name are the personal vibrational signature you chose for this life. Your birth date reveals what you are here to learn and the various cycles you will experience along the way, while your birth name says who you are and how you express yourself. Together, they are the compass heading of your life. The specific choices you make and route you take are up to you, but your vibrational signature will always help keep you on track.

Again, this is based upon the underlying spiritual belief that the day you were born and the name you were given were not by chance, but rather chosen by your own higher self to align with your planned energetic theme. Also, as an eternal spiritual being seeking as diverse a human experience as possible, you reincarnate many times to explore a wide range of themes, each time selecting a new birth date and name that vibrationally matches each particular theme. Thus, it is from these two numbers that you can obtain a comprehensive numerological profile of yourself and the life direction you chose this time around.

The format I developed for my readings is called the *Base-12 Numerology Road Map* and is the approach we will follow together in this book. There are sixteen numbers you will calculate in completing your Road Map: eight forecasting numbers derived from your birth date and the current, previous, and next year numbers as well as eight personality numbers derived from your birth name and current preferred name. These calculations and the road map they generate are presented in the next chapter.

Other Uses for Numerology

Much of what we have discussed thus far concerns number energies we cannot change, such as our birth date and birth name. So, let's wrap up our introduction to numerology with some numbers we *can* alter, including how we can select various names or numbers to provide a desired vibration at home and work.

Changing Your Current Name

While your birth name reflects who you came here to be, your current name is the name you use on a daily basis. Your current name acts like an additional vibrational tone played on top of the core tone of your birth name, and every time you use your current name, it alters how others perceive you and the types of experiences you attract.

Often we have several current names and alternate between them depending on the circumstances. For instance, a woman born as Catherine Jane Thomas may prefer to go by Catherine Thomas at work, Cathy Thomas in public, and Katie amongst close friends and family. Perhaps she's a public celebrity too and goes by the stage name of CJ Thomas. Each one of these names has a distinct vibe, so numerology is a great tool for understanding why we choose the names we do.

The current name we prefer, especially our first name, often changes too as we progress through different phases of our life. For example, the name *Bobby* may have felt right when a person was young and experiencing the informality and social conformance of childhood, but then his birth name of *Robert* resonated better once his focus turned to more adult themes of responsibility and authenticity.

Granted, the current name we adopt is not always entirely of our own choice, as in the case of married names when one spouse takes the surname of the other out of cultural convention. Still, those who come into our lives are always drawn to us as part of our personal learning and growth, and analyzing the numerological impact of using their last name will always reveal that underlying purpose.

Sometimes people go as far as changing their legal birth name too. But remember, you chose your birth name for a reason. It holds the vibrational map of who you want to be in this life and how you wish to express yourself. So, when a person dislikes the sound of their birth name, this is usually because there is an important aspect of themselves they are hesitant to face and have yet to do the inner work to understand and resolve it.

Some of our most powerful life lessons and catalysts for growth are those disguised by names or numbers (or people) we automatically dislike at first. So, numerology is as much about understanding why certain vibrations *don't* resonate with us as it is why other vibrations do.

Naming a Baby

Although you can certainly use numerology to select a baby name to match a certain vibe, I recommend against it. This, again, is because our birth name is the vibrational signature of who we are.

As such, parents-to-be should select a child's name based on what intuitively sounds and feels right and resist the temptation to "force" a vibration, such as an impressive-sounding master 22 or 33, that doesn't resonate with the baby's true nature. Remember, we are all connected in consciousness at our soul level, including the baby's higher self. Just trust the spiritual process to inspire you with the right name because I assure you it always will.

That said, once you do come up with one or more possible names that feel right, then certainly go ahead and check the numerological vibe they project and pick the one you like best. Don't be surprised if the alternate names you were considering end up with very similar numbers anyway!

Naming a Business

Numerology is extremely useful for identifying business names and names for products, services, or projects to resonate with a specific desired energy.

An example of a business aptly named for its company and products is Apple. The numerology of *Apple* is $1 + 7 + 7 + 3 + 5 = 23$ in base-10 $= 1\times12 +$

$\underline{11} = 1\underline{11} = 1 \times 12 + 0 = 1 + 0 = 1$ in base-12 and denoted as **10/1**, where 1 is the *outer* vibration of new beginnings, innovation, and leadership, and $1 + 0$ are the *inner* influences of new beginnings of potential. As such, the name *Apple* has the perfect vibration for this highly original and innovative market leader renowned for products that are all about personal empowerment.

Selecting an Address

Numerology is also useful for selecting addresses and locations to ensure that your home or office address, unit number, or floor resonates with the type of environment you prefer.

My home (and home office) address is 5674, which equals $5 + 6 + 7 + 4 = 22$ in base-10 and $1 \times 12 + \underline{10} = 1 + \underline{10} = \underline{11}$ in base-12 or **110/11**, which means illumination ($\underline{11}$) through new beginnings (1) of awareness ($\underline{10}$). My address has the right energy for providing an inspirational and illuminating setting for the intuitive nature of my work. The potential downside of this dynamic $\underline{11}$ vibe, however, is that it can make it easy to forget that my home is a place for relaxing too.

Choosing a Website Name

When choosing a website name, numerology is great for ensuring your name resonates with the type of work you do and clients you wish to attract. My website name of michaelsmith12 (excluding .com) equals 69 in base-10 and $5 \times 12 + 9 = 59$ in base-12, and this reduces to $5 + 9 = 1 \times 12 + 2 = 1 + 2 = 3$ or **12/3**. This perfectly matches my goal of being a catalyst (3) for exploring new beginnings (1) of physical-spiritual balance (2) through base-12 (12).

As you can see, lots of practical benefit can be gleaned from the numbers we are surrounded by in everyday life. They provide clarity to better navigate not only our own lives, but also to understand family, relationships, and work dynamics.

Despite having worked closely with numbers all my professional life as an engineer and statistician, I never realized just how limited my understanding actually was of the deeper energetic value and insight numbers possess.

Using Playing Cards as a Numerology Oracle Deck

The above examples show how versatile numerology is for determining the vibration of any number or name. Numerology when used as an oracle card deck is also very useful for gaining insight regarding any question you may have.

Maybe you wish to know more about a person you just met or a company you are considering working for. Perhaps you want to understand why a major event just happened in your life or why you seem to be attracting a certain repeating pattern of experiences. In this section we show how a regular deck of playing cards can be used as a powerful divination tool for pretty much any question you can think of.

Preparing Your Oracle Deck

How it works is to take any complete deck of playing cards and remove the Kings and Jokers. This leaves you with a forty-eight-card deck consisting of four duplicates of each of the following twelve cards: aces, jacks, queens, and the number cards from 2 to 10. Each of the twelve cards represents a single-digit number energy of the base-12 numerology cycle: the queen as 0, the ace as 1, each number card as its face value from 2 to <u>10</u>, and the jack as <u>11</u>.

As each type of card comes in two black suits and two red suits, the black cards represent a number's potential *positive qualities* while the red cards its *negative tendencies*. Together, these positive and negative traits represent the full vibrational personality of each number and are therefore neither good nor bad, simply different expressions of the number's range of potential to explore.

How to Ask Your Questions

The golden rule of Spirit/God/Source when answering our requests for higher guidance is that our free will is always respected. This applies to not only oracle and tarot card readings but any form of divination or spiritual inquiry, such as prayer, spiritual guidance readings, mediumship readings, or channeling. As such, the insights that numerology can provide are never to tell you *what to do* but rather to help you make more enlightened and empowered choices for yourself.

This means that *how* you ask your questions is important. So instead of asking for specific direction, such as *Should I do this?*, *Will this happen?*, and *Is this better than that?*, ask empowered questions, such as *Please provide insight into ...*, *What themes are playing out here?*, and *What is the main lesson being revealed by ...?* By asking your questions in this manner, with the intention of gaining insight rather than direction, you will always get the most out of numerology when used as an oracle tool.

Remember, we are all here to master our life lessons through our own discretion and intuition, not to have those choices made for us. And how you shuffle and mix the deck and select your cards is an intuitive choice. That's why it's helpful to relax each time you handle the cards and just go with the flow of what feels right. This allows your intuition to do its job in leading you to the appropriate cards which answer your question.

Types of Readings

There are many different ways you can use your homemade numerology deck to provide quick and easy insight and clarity into your life. Following are five types of readings you may find particularly useful, covering a broad range of situations you may encounter. These involve using single cards as representing single-digit numbers (the *outer energy* of a situation) or pairs of cards as two-digit numbers (the *inner influences* that contribute to a single-digit outer energy).

Step-by-step instructions are provided below.

Single Card Reading

If you wish to understand the overall energy of a given situation, person, place or thing, draw a single card and read its meaning using table 8 on pages 78–79.

1. Mix and shuffle the deck of cards.

2. While holding the card deck in your hand, ask your question (silently or out loud). Note that your question doesn't need to be limited to a single situation. You could instead ask for the energetic *difference* between two options.

45

3. Draw any card from the deck and place it faceup in front of you.

4. Read the meaning of the single-digit number in response to your question using table 8 on pages 78–79. If the card you draw is in a black suit, read the positive attributes of the number. If the card is in a red suit, read the negative tendencies.

Two-Card Comparison Reading (Two Cards Read Separately)

If you would like to compare the vibe between two options, circumstances or perspectives, draw a single card for each option and compare their respective meanings. This is useful in relationships for understanding how your vibe compares to another's, in decision-making to see how one option compares to a second, or to gain insight regarding the before-versus-after energy of a particular scenario.

1. Mix and shuffle the deck of cards.

2. While holding the card deck in your hand, ask (silently or out loud) what energy is held by the first of the two options you wish to compare.

3. Draw any card from the deck and place it faceup in front of you.

4. Now ask what energy is held by the second option you wish to compare.

5. Draw another card from the deck and place it faceup in front of you and to the right of your first card.

6. Read the meaning of the each of the two single-digit numbers using table 8 on pages 78–79 to see how they compare in terms of the energy they each hold. If a card is in a black suit, read the positive attributes of the number and if in a red suit, read its negative tendencies.

7. The numerical difference between the two numbers you draw reveals their *energetic* difference. This difference represents the type of energy that could bring the two sides into agreement (called a *bridge number* in numerology).

    • Say for example you draw the 6 of love and the 4 of structure. Their energetic difference is the 6 − 4 = 2 of duality. This means that the cautious and reserved 4 would need to express more of the social, outgoing and engaging nature of the 2 in order to project the loving and affectionate vibe of the 6 (i.e., 4 + 2 = 6). Similarly, the lovestruck and often self-sacrificing 6 needs to release some of the unbalanced, submissive and moody tendencies of the 2 in order to have the more stable, realistic and grounded attitude towards relationships of the 4 (i.e., 6 − 2 = 4).

Inner/Outer Energy Reading
(Two Cards Read Together as a Two-Digit Number)

If you seek deeper understanding of both the overall outer energy of your inquiry as well as the inner energies influencing it in the background, you can draw two cards as a two-digit number. This two-digit number when added together and reduced to a single digit (unless it is a twin-digit master number, such as 11, 22, or 33, which is not reduced) gives the overall outer energy, while the two individual card numbers reveal the inner influences working behind the scenes.

1. Mix and shuffle the deck of cards.

2. While holding the card deck in your hand, ask your question (silently or out loud). Note that your question doesn't need to be limited to a single situation. You could instead ask for the energetic difference between two options.

3. Draw any two cards from the deck. Place the first card faceup in front of you and the second card face-up to the right of the first card.

4. Look up the meaning of the two-digit number represented by your two cards (pages 101–148). This will describe the overall outer energy of your inquiry (the single digit your two-digit number reduces to) as well as the inner influences contributing to that outer energy (the face values of the two individual cards).

   If the number is not a master number:
   + If both cards you draw are in black suits, read the positive attributes.
   + If both cards you draw are in red suits, refer to the negative tendencies.
   + If one card is black and the other red, refer to the mixed meaning.

If the number is a master number (11, 22, 33, 44, 55, 66, 77, 88, 99, <u>10 10</u>, or <u>11 11</u>):

  • If both cards are black, read the positive meaning of the double-digit master number (e.g., positive qualities of 22).
  • If one card is black and the other red, refer to the positive meaning of the single-digit number the master number reduces to (e.g., positive qualities of 2 + 2 = 4).
  • If both cards are red, refer to the negative meaning of the single-digit number the master number reduces to (e.g., negative tendencies of 2 + 2 = 4).

Past/Present/Potential Timeline Reading
(Three Cards Read Separately)

If you would like to better understand the past, present and future potential that pertains to your question, you can draw three single cards for an overall snapshot of the timeline.

1. Mix and shuffle the deck of cards.

2. While holding the card deck in your hand, ask (silently or out loud) for three cards that describe the past, present, and future potential energy that pertains to your question.

3. Draw any three cards from the deck. Place the first card (past) faceup in front of you, the second card (present) faceup to the right of the first card, and the third card (potential) to the right of the second card.

4. Read the meaning of each of the three single-digit numbers using table 8 on pages 78–79 to see how the energy changes over the timeline from past to present to future. If a card is black read the positive attributes of the number and if red read its negative tendencies.

Inner/Outer Timeline Reading
(Three Pairs of Cards as Three Two-Digit Numbers)

If you would like to take an even closer look at the past, present, and future potential energy surrounding your question, you can draw three pairs of cards as three two-digit numbers. Each two-digit number when added together and reduced to a single digit gives the overall outer energy for the past, present, or future perspective, while the two individual digits within each pair of cards reveal the inner influences working behind the scenes.

1. Mix and shuffle the deck of cards.

2. While holding the card deck in your hand, ask (silently or out loud) for three pairs of cards that describe the past, present, and future potential pertaining to your question.

3. Draw any three pairs of cards from the deck. Place the first pair (past) face-up in front of you, the second pair (present) faceup to the right of the first pair and the third pair (future) to the right of the second pair.

4. Look up the meaning of each of the three two-digit numbers you drew (pages 101–148). Each will include the overall outer energy of your inquiry (the single digit your two-digit number reduces to) as well as the inner influences contributing to that outer energy (the face values of the two individual cards).

    If the number is not a master number:
    + If both cards you draw are in black suits, read the positive attributes.
    + If both cards you draw are in red suits, refer to the negative tendencies.
    + If one card is black and the other red, refer to the mixed meaning.

    If the number is a master number (11, 22, 33, 44, 55, 66, 77, 88, 99, <u>10 10</u>, or <u>11 11</u>):
    + If both cards are black, read the positive meaning of the double-digit master number (e.g., positive qualities of 22).

- If one card is black and the other red, refer to the positive meaning of the single-digit number the master number reduces to (e.g., positive qualities of $2 + 2 = 4$).
- If both cards are red, refer to the negative meaning of the single-digit number the master number reduces to (e.g., negative tendencies of $2 + 2 = 4$).

5. Read the meanings for each of the three pairs of cards from left to right to see how the energy changes over the timeline from past to present to future.

3

HOW TO CALCULATE
YOUR NUMBERS

With the basics of base-12 numerology under your belt, you are now ready to put that knowledge to work in this chapter by preparing your own personal numerology reading.

The format we will use for your reading is called the *Base-12 Numerology Road Map*. I call it a road map because it highlights the overall life path you chose for this journey (through your birth date) and the major lessons, opportunities, and obstacles you want to encounter along the way in mastering your driving skills. It also indicates what type of driver you want to be (through your birth name), right down to your personality, desires, strengths, and weaknesses.

Your road map is composed of sixteen numbers that we will explain and calculate together as we go, with plenty of examples. These include your eight forecasting numbers derived from your birth date and eight personality numbers from your birth name.

Written in the style of a trip itinerary, your road map is a quick and easy fill-in-the-blank document. It consists of three parts: the first part is where you enter your personal information, the second part is the worksheet where you calculate your numbers, and the last part is where you transfer your numbers and add their meanings (covered in the next chapter). You can find a blank copy in the appendix.

Forecasting Numbers

Within your *forecasting numbers* are eight types of numbers we will calculate. Your life path number is the most important of these, as it indicates your overall goal for this life. The other seven numbers reveal what you can expect to experience at various stages to help you achieve that goal. These include your growth cycles, pinnacle and challenge cycles, birth day number, maturity number, world year number, and personal year number.

Life Path Number

Calculated from your full birth date, your *life path number* is your life purpose, the overall theme and lessons you are here to explore. All the other numbers in your numerology road map play a supporting role in helping you achieve this overall theme.

A common misconception in numerology is that the life path number is all you really need to know, just as many believe their sun sign in astrology is enough to understand themselves fully. This is far from the case. Your life path is only the starting point.

How to Calculate Your Life Path Number

First, convert each of the three numbers of your birth date (month, day, year) to base-12 using table 5 (page 37) and table 6 (page 38), then reduce each number to a single digit (unless you get a master number like 11 or 22).

Next, add your three base-12 numbers together. If the sum is a single digit between 1 and <u>11</u>, this is your life path number. If the sum is not a single digit, keep reducing until you get a single digit.

For example, let's use my birth date of January 26, 1963:

	Base-10		Base-12		10s	1s
Month:	1	$\rightarrow$	1	$\rightarrow$	-	1
Day:	26	$\rightarrow$	22	$\rightarrow$	2x12	2
Year:	1963	$\rightarrow$	5	$\rightarrow$	-	5

First Reduction: 2x12 + 8 = **28** (not a single digit)

$\downarrow$

Second Reduction: 2 + 8 = **10** (single digit)

Therefore, my life path number is **28/10.**

Your life path number, like every other number you'll calculate in your road map, will either be the result of adding together two other single digits (as in our example of 2 + 8 = **10**,) or it will be a single digit directly, not requiring this extra step.

Note that when adding your numbers together, make sure you add the ones column first in case you reach 12 and have to carry a 1 to the tens column (we don't have to worry about that here since 1 + 2 + 5 = 8).

Growth Cycles

Calculated from your birth month, day, and year, your *growth cycle numbers* are the three specific themes you will explore over your life time, and they span the main stages of your life: youth, midlife, and later years. They combine to give the overall vibration of your life path. Thus, the more you are able to learn and grow through each cycle, the more you will have achieved your life path. Or another way of putting it, the "journey" (of the three growth cycles) is more important than the "destination" (the life path) because they are vibrationally one and the same.

Also keep in mind that even if the various themes of your three growth cycles seem very different and unrelated, they were specifically chosen by you to complement each other and to cover all the bases you set out to examine.

You will have already determined your three growth cycles in the first step of your life path calculation, but let's cover them again here individually and in more detail.

How to Calculate Your First Growth Cycle

This is your month of birth, and the cycle begins the time you are born and ends in thirty-six years minus your life path number. As such, this is the theme you will experience most strongly in youth.

To find, convert your birth month to base-12 using table 5 (page 37), then reduce to a single digit.

How to Calculate Your Second Growth Cycle (and Birth Day Number)

This is your day of birth and spans from the end of your first cycle until twenty-seven years later. As such, this theme will be felt most strongly during your working years. This is also called your *birth day number* as it highlights a special talent you possess to assist you with your life path, particularly in your career.

To find, convert your birth day to base-12 using table 5 (page 37), then reduce to a single digit (unless you get a master number like 11 or 22, which is not reduced further).

How to Calculate Your Third Growth Cycle

This is your year of birth and lasts from the end of your second cycle through the rest of your life. As such, this is the main theme you will explore in your later years.

To find, convert your birth year to base-12 using table 6 (page 38), then reduce to a single digit (unless you get a master number like 11 or 22, which is not reduced further).

Continuing our previous example using my birth date of January 26, 1963, here is how my three cycles would be calculated:

First Growth Cycle: Birth month = **1**. Age range: **0 to 26** (since 36 – life path = 36 – 10 = 26)

Second Growth Cycle: Birth day = 26 in base-10 = **22** in base-12. Age range: **26 to 53** (26 + 27 = 53)

Third Growth Cycle: Birth year = 1963 in base-10 = **14/5** in base-12. Age range: **53+**

Pinnacle Cycles

Your *pinnacles cycles*, like your growth cycles, are again based upon the numbers of your birth date, but this time through various pairings of your month, day, and year. Also like your growth cycles, each of your pinnacle cycles lasts for a certain number of years. Note that any master numbers, such as 11, 22, or 33, that occur in your birth date are reduced this time to single digits before calculating the cycles.

You can think of your pinnacle cycles as four periods of opportunity and advancement you will experience to help you achieve your life path. The types of opportunities you encounter in each pinnacle cycle will be of a particular theme, one that will use your natural talents in support of your forward progress during that stage of your life. We don't enter any incarnation with the expectation of failure, so we place enough bread crumbs in the form of pinnacles to help find our way.

How to Calculate Your First Pinnacle Cycle

This is calculated by adding together your month of birth and day of birth. It begins the time you are born and ends when you are thirty-six minus your life path number. Note that for all your pinnacle cycles, any master numbers, such as 11, 22, or 33, that occur in your birth date *are* reduced to single digits before calculating the cycles.

To find, convert the sum of your birth month and birth day to base-12 using table 5 on (page 37), then reduce to a single digit.

How to Calculate Your Second Pinnacle Cycle

This is calculated by adding your day of birth and year of birth and lasts nine years from the end of the first pinnacle.

To find, convert the sum of your birth day and birth year to base-12 using table 5, then reduce to a single digit.

How to Calculate Your Third Pinnacle Cycle

This is calculated by adding your *first pinnacle number* to your *second pinnacle number* and lasts nine years after the second pinnacle.

To find, convert the sum of your *first pinnacle* and *second pinnacle* to base-12 using table 5, then reduce to a single digit.

How to Calculate Your Fourth Pinnacle Cycle

This is calculated by adding your month of birth to your year of birth and lasts from the end of the third pinnacle to the end of your life.

To find, convert the sum of your birth month and birth year to base-12 using table 5, then reduce to a single digit.

Challenge Cycles

During each of your four pinnacle cycles, you will also encounter a specific *challenge* theme you will need to overcome in order to take advantage of the opportunities presented by your pinnacle theme.

Each challenge is typically an unresolved weakness or fear that you wish to address in this life. As such, each pinnacle-challenge pair presents a vibrational tug-of-war of sorts, testing your resolve to stretch yourself and work through obstacles in achieving what you desire. In this way, your pinnacle and challenge themes work together to give you extra incentive in the form of opportunities to conquer your fears provoked by the challenges.

First Challenge Cycle

This is calculated by subtracting your day of birth from your month of birth and lasts from the time you are born until 36 years minus your life path.

Subtract your birth month from your birth day, convert the answer to base-12 using table 5 on (page 37), then reduce to a single digit.

As with the pinnacle cycles, any master numbers, such as 11, 22, or 33, that occur in your birth date *are* reduced to single digits before calculating the cycles. Also, ignore any negative sign when calculating your challenge cycles.

Second Challenge Cycle

This is calculated by subtracting your year of birth from your day of birth and lasts 9 years from the end of the first challenge.

Subtract your birth day from your birth year, convert the answer to base-12 using table 5, then reduce to a single digit.

Third Challenge Cycle

This is calculated by subtracting your *second challenge cycle* from your *first challenge cycle* and lasts 9 years from the end of the *second challenge cycle*.

Subtract your *first challenge cycle* from your *second challenge cycle*, convert the answer to base-12 using table 5, then reduce to a single digit.

Fourth Challenge Cycle

This is calculated by subtracting your year of birth from your month of birth and lasts from the end of the third challenge.

Subtract your birth month from your birth year, convert the answer to base-12 using table 5 on, then reduce to a single digit.

For example, my pinnacles and challenges would be calculated as follows:

First Pinnacle Cycle: birth month + day = 1 + 4 = **5**
First Challenge Cycle: birth month − day = 1 − 4 = **3**
Age range: **0 to 26** (since 36 − life path = 36 − <u>10</u> = 26)

Second Pinnacle Cycle: birth day + year = 4 + 5 = **9**
Second Challenge Cycle: birth day − year = 4 − 5 = **1**
Age range: **26 to 35** (since first cycle + 9 = 26 + 9 = 35)

Third Pinnacle Cycle: first pinnacle + second pinnacle = 5 + 9 = 14 in base-10 = **12/3** in base-12

Third Challenge Cycle: first challenge – second challenge = 3 – 1 = **2**

Age range: **35 to 44** (since second cycle + 9 = 35 + 9 = 44)

Fourth Pinnacle Cycle: birth month + year = 1 + 5 = **6**

Fourth Challenge Cycle: birth month – year = 1 –5 = **4**

Age range: **44+**

Maturity Number

Your *maturity number* is the last of your eight forecasting numbers and is the only one that requires one of your personality numbers, your expression number, in order to calculate it.

The sum of your life path and expression numbers, your maturity number is the primary goal and interest for the second half of your life, after age thirty-five. It is felt most strongly later in life because by then you have experienced many of your lessons (life path) while learning to express yourself authentically (expression number). You thus become a vibrational blend of the two.

This is why career interests and relationship dynamics often change as we approach mid-life, sometimes dramatically. I'm a good example of this. With a 28/<u>10</u> life path and a 17/8 expression number, I was very career-driven and focused on the 8 theme of physical manifestation and abundance. Then my maturity number of 16/7 kicked in and my focus rapidly shifted to the 7 theme of spiritual truth, the same time I had my spiritual awakening. I also admittedly became a much more compassionate and open person, softened by the 1 + 6 of new beginnings of love and harmony.

How to Calculate Your Maturity Number

Add your life path number and your expression number together, convert the sum to base-12, and reduce using table 5 (page 37).

For example, let's use my base-12 life path of 28/10 and expression number of 17/8:

Maturity Number = life path + expression

$$= 28/\underline{10} + 17/8$$
$$= \underline{10} + 8 = 18 \text{ in base-10}$$
$$= 1\text{x}12 + 6 = 16 \text{ in base-12}$$
$$= 1 + 6 = 7 \text{ or } \mathbf{16/7}, \text{ which is my maturity number}$$

World Year and Personal Year

You can also utilize numerology to forecast the energy to expect for an upcoming day, month, or year and to review prior periods to better understand what happened and why. The *world year* and *personal year* are perhaps the most important forecasting energies we should know, as they provide a heads-up about the overall energy theme we will experience any given year. This enables us to anticipate what to expect, both globally and personally, and thereby make the most of our efforts from one year to the next.

I like to include the prior year, current year, and upcoming year in the Base-12 Numerology Road Map, as those are the most relevant to the near-term in helping us understand and navigate the broader energetic landscape.

Based upon any year of interest, the world year number is the overall theme everyone experiences during that year. Although you won't typically feel the vibration of the world year number very strongly personally (unless it matches your life path or personal year number), it is nevertheless a good indicator of the types of global events, trends, and patterns to expect.

Based upon the sum of your birth month, birth day, and any given world year, the personal year number is the overall theme you will personally experience that year. This number will have a significant impact on you each year, particularly if it matches your life path or the current growth cycle you are in. When it does match, you will encounter circumstances and events that directly relate to why you are here and the specific lessons you wish to learn. Such years can feel particularly intense yet productive.

How to Calculate the World Year and Personal Year Numbers

As with your pinnacle and challenge cycles, any master number that may occur in your year of birth is reduced to a single digit when calculating the year energies.

World Year: Convert the year of interest to base-12 and reduce per table 6 (page 38).

Personal Year: Add together your birth month, birth day, and world year number, convert the sum to base-12, and reduce using table 5 (page 37).

Here are a few examples of how to calculate a personal year using my birth month and day:

2019 in base-12 is a **6** world year

personal year = birth month + birth day + world year
$$= 1 + 22 + 6 \text{ in base-12} = 1 + 4 + 6 = \underline{\mathbf{11}} \text{ personal year}$$

2020 in base-12 is a **7** world year

personal year = birth month + birth day + world year
$$= 1 + 22 + 7 \text{ in base-12} = 1 + 4 + 7 = 1\text{x}12+0 \text{ in base-10}$$
$$= 10 \text{ in base-12} = 1 + 0 = 1 \text{ for a } \mathbf{10/1} \text{ personal year}$$

2021 in base-12 is an **8** world year

personal year = birth month + birth day + world year
$$= 1 + 22 + 8 \text{ in base-12} = 1 + 4 + 8 = 1\text{x}12 + 1 \text{ in base-10}$$
$$= 11 \text{ in base-12 for a } \mathbf{11} \text{ personal year}$$

The Personality Numbers

Within the personality numbers, there are eight numbers that will be included in your road map. These include your expression number, soul number, personality number, bridge number, balance number, hidden passions, karmic lessons, and current name number. All based upon the vibrational qualities of your name, these numbers provide insight regarding your strengths, weaknesses, inner motivations, and outer behaviors and how you can manage them to your best advantage.

Expression Number

Based upon the sum of the letter energies in your full birth name, your *expression number* indicates who you are, your general direction in life, and your born talents, traits ,and preferences to express in exploring your life path.

As such, your best career choice will be one that matches the theme of your expression number, as it will feel like a calling rather than a job and will bring out the best in you. Also, just as your life path is the vibrational sum of your three growth cycles, your expression number is the sum of your soul number (vowels in your birth name) and personality number (consonants in your birth name). These two numbers we introduce next.

How to Calculate Your Expression Number

The first step is to convert the letters in each of your birth names into numbers using table 1 (page 30), sum the numbers of each name, then convert and reduce each sum to base-12 using table 5 on page 37.

For example, we'll use my birth name of *Michael Peter Smith*:

Michael = 4 + 9 + 3 + 8 + 1 + 5 + 3 = 33 in base-10 = 2x12 + 9 = 29 in base-12 = 2 + 9 = <u>11</u> or 29/<u>**11**</u>

Peter = 7 + 5 + 2 + 5 + 9 = 28 in base-10 = 2x12 + 4 = 24 in base-12 = 2 + 4 = 6 or 24/**6**

Smith = 1 + 4 + 9 + 2 + 8 = 24 in base-10 = 2x12 + 0 = 20 in base-12 = 2 + 0 = 2 or 20/**2**

Remember to use your birth name exactly as shown on your birth certificate, including any multiple middle names and last names. A compound or hyphenated last name, such as Jones-Smith, is treated as a single last name and any suffix, such as Jr. (Junior), Sr. (Senior), or III (the Third), is excluded. Also, don't worry if you don't have a middle name. Your birth name, whatever form it takes, was the beginning vibration you chose because it matches your true vibration.

The second step is to add your base-12 numbers together (final digits only), then convert that sum to base-12 and reduce using table 5.

$\underline{11} + 6 + 2 = 19$ in base-10

$= 1\text{x}12 + 7 = 17$ in base-12

$= 1 + 7 = 8$ or $\mathbf{17/8}$, which is my expression number

Soul Number

Based upon the sum of the letter energies of the vowels in your birth name, your *soul number* is what motivates and fulfills you inside.

When you are expressing yourself in line with your soul number by pursuing your true passions, you feel a deep sense of joy and satisfaction. Conversely, when you are not doing what you love, you feel uninspired and unfulfilled.

How to Calculate Your Soul Number

The first step is to convert the vowels in each of your birth names into numbers using table 1 (page 30), sum the numbers of each name, then convert and reduce each sum to base-12 using table 5 (page 37). Here's an example using my name, Michael Peter Smith, again:

$\text{IAE} + \text{EE} + \text{I} = (9 + 1 + 5) + (5 + 5) + 9$

$= 15 + 10 + 9$ in base-10

$= 1\text{x}12 + 3 + 10 + 9 = 13 + \underline{10} + 9$ in base-12

$= (1 + 3) + \underline{10} + 9 = \mathbf{4} + \underline{\mathbf{10}} + \mathbf{9}$

The second step is to add your base-12 single digit numbers together, then convert your sum to base-12 and reduce again using table 5.

$4 + \underline{10} + 9 = 23$ in base-10

$= 1\text{x}12 + 11 = 1\underline{11}$ in base-12

$= 1 + \underline{11} = 12$ in base-10

$$= 1 \times 12 + 0 = 10 \text{ in base-12}$$
$$= 1 + 0 = 1 \text{ or } \mathbf{10/1}, \text{ which is my soul number}$$

Personality Number

Based upon the sum of the letter energies of the consonants in your birth name, your *personality number* is how others perceive you and what you allow others to see. The personality number therefore can be considered the "outer you" while your soul number is the "inner you."

For instance, if you seem to come across wrong quite often in social settings and are frequently misunderstood, it is likely that your personality and soul numbers are distinctly different. Basically, how others see you isn't how you want to be seen. This can be remedied though, thanks to your bridge number.

How to Calculate Your Personality Number

The first step is to convert the consonants in each of your birth names into numbers using table 1 (page 30), sum the numbers of each name, then convert and reduce each sum to base-12 using table 5 (page 37). Here's an example using my name:

$$\text{MCHL} + \text{PTR} + \text{SMTH} = (4 + 3 + 8 + 3) + (7 + 2 + 9) + (1 + 4 + 2 + 8)$$
$$= 18 + 18 + 15 \text{ in base-10}$$
$$= (1 \times 12 + 6) + (1 \times 12 + 6) + 1 \times 12 + 3) = 16$$
$$+ 16 + 13 \text{ in base-12}$$
$$= (1 + 6) + (1 + 6) + (1 + 3) = 7 + 7 + 4$$

The second step is to add your base-12 numbers together (final digits only), then convert your sum to base-12 and reduce again using table 5.

$$7 + 7 + 4 = 18 \text{ in base-10}$$
$$= 1 \times 12 + 6 = 16 \text{ in base-12}$$
$$= 1 + 6 = 7 \text{ or } \mathbf{16/7} \text{ which is my personality number}$$

Bridge Number

Based upon the difference between your soul number and personality number, the *bridge number* highlights how you can close the gap between your outer personality and the real you inside—essentially how to be more authentic.

For example, if you have a conservative and risk-averse personality number of 4 but a loving and giving soul number of 6, your bridge number is the social and relationship-seeking 2 (4 − 6). This means that you need to put yourself out there more and socially interact so that you can learn to loosen up and allow others to see your loving nature. Note that we are just interested here in the relative difference between your soul and personality numbers, so just ignore any negative sign after subtracting.

How to Calculate Your Bridge Number

Subtract your soul number from your personality number, convert to base-12, and reduce using table 5 (page 37). For example, here's my bridge number calculation:

bridge number = soul number—personality number = $1 - 7 = 6$

Balance Number

Based upon the first initials of your birth name, the *balance number* reveals how you react to difficult situations. Just as your first initials are the first impression of your written name, how you respond under stress is your emotional first impression to others.

My balance number, for example, is the 1 of independence and control. This indicates that my first reaction under pressure is to want to isolate myself from the situation and impatiently take matters into my own hands. So true!

How to Calculate Your Balance Number

Convert the first initials of each of your birth names into numbers using table 1 (page 30), add them together and convert the sum to its reduced base-12 form using table 5 (page 37).

For example: M + P + S = 4 + 7 + 1 = 12 in base-10

$$= 1 \times 12 + 0 = 10 \text{ in base-12}$$

$$= 1 + 0 = 1 \text{ or } \mathbf{10/1}, \text{ which is my } \textit{balance number}$$

Hidden Passions

Your *hidden passions* are those letter energies in your birth name that repeat most often (three or more times) and represent your strongest talents to utilize to your advantage. As your name resonates powerfully with those particular energies, you naturally attract situations and experiences which draw upon those gifts.

Hidden passions are generally themes you have mastered well in prior lives and therefore do not require as much "remedial work" to explore further. Occasionally, however, we may continue developing a strength over multiple lives if mastery and its associated lessons is our goal. This I believe is the case with child prodigies who are born as highly skilled artists, musicians, athletes, or linguists.

How to Calculate Your Hidden Passion numbers

The most frequently repeating numbers (letter energies) in your birth name. For example, in Michael Peter Smith (4938153 75259 14928), the number of times each number energy appears is given below:

1: appears 2 times

2: appears 2 times

3: appears 2 times

4: appears 2 times

5: appears 3 times

6: missing

7: appears 1 time

8: appears 2 times

9: appears 3 times

As the most frequently occurring number energies in my name are 5 and 9, each appearing three times, those are my *hidden passions*.

Karmic Lessons

Your *karmic lessons* are letter energies missing from your birth name. These represent incomplete lessons from your prior lives that you wish to resolve or specific themes you want to explore this time around. As such, these are vibrational "gaps" you intentionally placed in your name so that they surface as weaknesses requiring you to dig deeply and consciously work to learn about those themes.

Even if you don't happen to have any *karmic lesson numbers*, you will still experience challenges through the rest of your numbers as a necessary part of your growth. The only difference is that you won't feel these challenges as distinct personal weaknesses in the way that *karmic lessons* feel. Also, the influence of a *karmic lesson number* is reduced when it also appears elsewhere in your numbers.

How to Calculate Your Karmic Lesson Number

Note numbers (letter energies) missing from your birth name. For example, the only number energy missing from Michael Peter Smith is 6, so 6 is my *karmic lesson*.

Current Name Number

Your *current name number* is the first and last name you go by on a daily basis, such as an abbreviated first name you prefer or married last name. As discussed earlier on page 41 in the section "Changing Your Current Name", the current name you use projects a different vibration than your full birth name and therefore attracts different experiences.

How to Calculate Your Current Name Number

The first step is to convert the letters in each of your daily names into numbers using table 1 on page 30, sum the numbers of each name, then convert and reduce each sum to base-12 using table 5 (page 37).

For example, I usually go by the name *Michael Smith* on a daily basis:

Michael Smith = (4 + 9 + 3 + 8 + 1 + 5 + 3) + (1 + 4 + 9 + 2 + 8) = 33 + 24 in base-10

$$= (2 \times 12 + 9) + (2 \times 12 + 0) = 29 + 20 \text{ in base-12}$$

$$= (2 + 9) + (2 + 0) = \underline{11} + 2$$

Next, add your base-12 numbers together (final digits only), then convert that sum to base-12 and reduce using table 5 (page 37).

$\underline{11}$ + 2 = 13 in base-10

$$= 1 \times 12 + 1 = \mathbf{11} \text{ in base-12 (master number, so not reduced further)}$$

So, master number 11 is my current name number.

Completing Your Base-12 Numerology Road Map

The sixteen numbers we just calculated, your eight forecasting numbers and eight personality numbers, are everything you need to complete your personal numerology reading. As mentioned, the format we will use for putting together your reading is called the Base-12 Numerology Road Map.

The road map reads like a letter to yourself; a personal treasure map you created prior to your birth, patiently waiting to be opened when you are ready. Full of wise and loving guidance from the one who knows you best, your higher self, your road map describes who you are, what you set out to learn in this life, and how you can make the most of the adventure. The fact you're reading this book now means the time has come for you to open your road map and benefit from the insights your numerology reveals.

The road map document is designed to be simple to use and easy to understand, consisting of an eight-page template that already spells out what every type of number means. All you need to do is to fill in the blanks to make it all about you! There are just three steps involved:

Step 1: Enter your basic personal information on page 187, including your full birth name, the current name you go by on a daily basis, and your birth date.

Step 2: Complete the calculation worksheet on pages 188–89 for your sixteen numbers, using table 1 (pages 30) to look up the letter energies of your names and table 5 and table 6 (pages 37 and 38) for the base-12 conversions of any numbers you may come across.

Step 3: Enter your sixteen numbers on pages 190–194, along with their meanings from table 8 (pages 78–79) and table 9 (pages 89–90).

Shown below for illustration purposes is what a completed road map looks like, using the sample calculations we just walked through of yours truly. A blank version of the road map is included at the end of the book in the appendix (and on my website at www.michaelsmith12.com) to give you working copies to play with.

Once you finish your own road map and see how quick and easy it is, I encourage you to do those of your family and closest friends. Not only is it a lot of fun to compare numbers, but very informative too. That's because the people closest to you are all part of your "soul family." Each one of them agreed to incarnate alongside you to play various supporting roles to your journey, just as you agreed to support theirs. Knowing their road maps will reveal how you are all connected in this life time and how you are meant to complement one another in transformative ways.

My Base-12 Numerology Road Map

Birth Name: _____**Michael**_____ _____**Peter**_____ _____**Smith**_____
                    first   *middle*   *last*

Current Name: _____**Michael**_____ _____**Smith**_____
                        first   *last*

Birth Date: _____**January**_____ __**26**__ _____**1963**_____
                      month   *day*   *year*

Numerology is based upon the principle that everything is energy and has a vibrational character, including numbers, letters, and words. My birth date and birth name are the personal vibrational signature I chose for this life. My birth date reveals what I am here to learn and the various cycles I will experience along the way (forecasting numbers), while my birth name says who I am and how I express myself (personality numbers). Together, they are the compass heading of my life. The specific choices I make and route I take are up to me, but my vibrational signature will always help keep me on course.

The vibrational road map I have chosen for this journey is revealed in my base-12 numerology, where every experience, relationship, or incarnation follows a universal cycle of twelve vibrational themes from the 0 of potential to the 11 of illumination. How fully I explore each experience determines how fully I may learn the lessons contained within.

Calculation Worksheet

My Base-12 Numerology Road Map and all the insights it reveals about me are based upon my eight forecasting numbers and eight personality numbers, calculated on the next two pages.

Forecasting Numbers from My Birth Date

	Birth Month	Birth Day	Birth Year
	1	26	1963
3 Growth Cycles:	1st = **1**	2nd = **22**	3rd = 1177 = **14/5**
age range:	0 to 26 yrs	26 to 53 yrs	53 yrs +
		Special talent	

Life Path	1 + 22 + 5 = **28/10**	What you are here to learn, overall theme to explore
Maturity Number LP + Expr = **10** + 8 = **16/7**		Your major goal & direction for adulthood (35+yrs)

	1st cycle	2nd cycle	3rd cycle	4th cycle	
4 Pinnacle Cycles:	mo + dy = 1 + 4 = **5**	dy + yr = 4 + 5 = **9**	1st + 2nd = 5 + 9 = **12/3**	mo + yr = 1 + 5 = **6**	4 periods of opportunity
4 Challenge Cycles:	mo − dy = 1 − 4 = **3**	dy − yr = 4 − 5 = **1**	1st − 2nd = 3 − 1 = **2**	mo − yr = 1 − 5 = **4**	4 periods of challenge
age range:	0 to 26 yrs	26 to 35 yrs	35 to 44 yrs	44+ yrs	

	Prior Year	Current Year	Next Year	
	2018	**2019**	**2020**	
World Year:	1202 = **5**	1203 = **6**	1204 = **7**	Energetic theme everyone experiences that year
Personal Year:	1 + 4 + 5 = **10**	1 + 4 + 6 = **11**	1 + 4 + 7 = **10/1**	Energetic theme you experience that year

Personality Numbers from My Birth Name

	First Birth Name	Middle Birth Name	Last Birth Name		
all letters:	**Michael** 4938153 = **29/11**	**Peter** 75259 = **24/6**	**Smith** 14928 = **20/2**	=	**Expression Number** $\underline{11}+6+2 = $ **17/8** — *How you can best express who you are, your calling*
vowels:	IAE = 915 = **13/4**	EE = 55 = **10**	I = **9**	=	**Soul Number** $4+\underline{10}+9 = $ **10/1** — *Your inner yearning*
consonants:	MCHL = 4383 = **16/7**	PTR = 729 = **16/7**	SMTH = 1428 = **13/4**	=	**Personality Number** $7+7+4 = $ **16/7** — *Your outer personality*
					Bridge Number Soul − Pers = $1-7 = $ **6** — *How to bridge your inner and outer self to be authentic*
initials:	M = 4	P = 7	S = 1	=	**Balance Number** $4+7+1 = $ **10/1** — *How you react to difficult situations*
to 9 occurrences in full birth name:	**Karmic Lessons** missing = **6** *Prior life lesson or weakness to address*	**fair** once = 7	**proficient** twice = 1, 2, 3, 4, 8		**Hidden Passions** 3x or more = **5, 9** — *Your greatest strengths*

	Current First Name		Current Last Name		
	Michael 4938153 = **29/11**		**Smith** 14928 = **20/2**	=	**Current Name Number** $\underline{11}+2 = $ **11** — *The vibration your current name projects*

0	1	2	3	4	5	6	7	8	9	10	11	11	22	33
Potential	A	B	C	D	E	F	G	H	I	Awareness	Illumination	Mastery of Self	Mastery of Duality	Master of Catalyst
	J	K	L	M	N	O	P	Q	R					
	S	T	U	V	W	X	Y	Z						
New Beginnings	Duality	Catalyst	Structure	Change	Love	Truth	Manifestation	Completion						

Table 7. Number and Letter Meanings

Forecasting Numbers from My Birth Date: "My Path"

My *life path* (based on my birth date) is the overall theme and major lessons I have chosen to explore and involves learning about 28/10. This *life path* indicates I will learn about the theme of awareness (10) through the duality (2) of manifestation and abundance (8).

I will experience this theme over three *growth cycles*, each with its own timing and focus:

1. My *first growth cycle* (based on my birth month) will last roughly from birth to age twenty-six with a focus on the 1 theme of new beginnings (1).

2. My *second growth cycle* (birth day) will last about twenty-seven years, from age twenty-six to fifty-three and will focus on the 22 master number theme of mastery of duality (22). Also called my *birth day number*, this is a special talent I possess to help me navigate my *life path*.

3. My *third growth cycle* (birth year) will last from about age fifty-three through the rest of my life, with a focus on the 14/5 theme of change (5) through new beginnings (1) of structure and stability (4).

There are two other types of cycles generated from my birth date: four *pinnacle cycles* that bring periods of opportunity and four *challenge cycles* that present challenges to overcome in pursuing those opportunities:

1. My *first pinnacle cycle* (birth month plus birth day) will occur from birth to age twenty-six, bringing opportunities involving the theme of change (5). But to take advantage of this, I need to overcome my *first challenge cycle* theme (birth month minus birth day) involving challenges of catalysts (3).

2. My *second pinnacle cycle* (birth day plus birth year) will last nine years from age twenty-six to thirty-five and will present opportunities involving the theme of completion (9). But to take advantage of this, I need to overcome my *second challenge cycle* theme (birth day minus year) involving challenges of new beginnings (1).

3. My *third pinnacle cycle* (first pinnacle plus second pinnacle) will last another nine years from age thirty-five to forty-four, with opportunities involving the 12/3 theme of catalysts (3) through new beginnings (1) of duality (2). But to take advantage of this, I need to overcome my *third challenge cycle* theme (*first challenge* minus *second challenge*) involving challenges of duality (2).

4. My *fourth pinnacle cycle* (birth month plus birth year) will last from age forty-four through the rest of my life, with opportunities involving the theme of love and harmony (6). But to take advantage of this, I will need to overcome my *fourth challenge cycle* theme (birth month minus birth year) which involves challenges of structure and stability (4).

My *maturity number* is the sum of my *life path* and *expression number* and indicates the main direction for the second half of my life (after age thirty-five). As my *maturity number* is 16/7, I will focus on spiritual truth and knowledge (7) through new beginnings (1) of love and harmony (6).

Each year also has its own energetic theme that influences our own personal vibe during the full twelve months. The *world year* affects everyone with the same overall theme, while our *personal year* (year of interest plus birth month plus birth day) is how we personally feel that year's effect. Following are those numbers for last year, this year, and next year:

- Last year, 2019, was a *world year* of love and harmony (6). For me, it was a *personal year* of illumination (<u>11</u>).

- This year, 2020, is a *world year* of spiritual truth and knowledge (7). For me, it is a 10/1 *personal year* of new beginnings (1) through new beginnings (1) of potential (0).
- Next year, 2021, will be a *world year* of manifestation and abundance (8). For me, it will be a *personal year* of self-mastery (11).

Personality Numbers from My Birth Name: "Who I Am"

My birth name reveals that my *expression number* is 17/8. This means that I can best express my true self and potential in areas involving manifestation and abundance (8) through new beginnings (1) of spiritual truth and knowledge (7).

The vowels of my birth name reveal my *soul number*, my soul's inner yearning. As my *soul number* is 10/1, my inner yearning is for new beginnings (1) through new beginnings (1) of potential (0).

Likewise, the consonants in my birth name give my *personality number*, my outer personality of how I am perceived by others. The energy I project is the 16/7 vibration of spiritual truth and knowledge (7) through new beginnings (1) of love and harmony (6).

The difference between my *soul* and *personality numbers* is my *bridge number*. This indicates how I can adjust my outer behavior (personality) to better align with how I see myself (soul), how to be perceived as authentic. My *bridge number* is 6, so embodying the positive qualities of this number of love, harmony and compassion reveals my soul's true nature.

How I react in difficult situations is my *balance number* and is given by the first initials of my birth name. My *balance number* is 10/1, so under pressure I tend to isolate myself from the situation and impatiently take matters into my own hands.

The number of times each letter-number energy from 1 to 9 appears in my birth name indicates my relative strengths and weaknesses at this point in my soul's development. Those appearing three or more times are considered my *hidden passions*, my strengths. For me, these include change (5) and completion (9). As such, I have the positive qualities of the 5 vibration of adaptability, courage, and trust and the positive qualities of the 9 vibration of contentment, dedication, and humanitarianism.

Any letter-number missing from my birth name is a *karmic lesson* and highlights a specific weakness or unresolved lesson carried over from my prior lives. By choosing a birth name missing the letter vibrations of my *karmic lessons*, I will feel its absence and the need to work at it as a priority for this life. My *karmic lesson* is 6, which involves learning to be more loving, accepting, and compassionate to myself and others.

The last of the numbers in my *Base-12 Numerology Road Map* is my *current name number*. Although my full birth name (*expression number*) reflects who I truly am, the current name I use can adjust that vibration and the energy it projects. My current name of *Michael Smith* projects the 11 master number vibration of mastery of self (11).

WHAT THE NUMBERS MEAN

In this chapter, you will learn what all the numbers mean with examples show-ing how the meanings are applied. We begin with the single-digit numbers from 0 to <u>11</u>. In addition to the general meaning of each number, every odd number also has a masculine personality and every even number a feminine vibe. We discuss how numbers can work together to maintain a masculine-feminine bal-ance or clash if that balance is ignored.

We then cover the meanings of the master numbers from 11 to <u>11 11</u>. This includes an explanation of the greater clarity provided to the master numbers in base-12 than base-10. With a handle on what the numbers mean, we will examine how they all fit together through the base-12 numerology cycle. This brings us to the concept of the *Path of Resonance*, the ideal vibrational path we can take through the base-12 cycle if we experience each number's theme at its most balanced and natural level.

The rest of the chapter provides the detailed meanings of all the numbers, with a section dedicated to each number. This includes the specialized mean-ings for each number based on all possible combinations of two-digit *inner in-fluence* numbers that add together to give that single-digit *outer* number.

What the Single-Digit Numbers Mean from 0 to <u>11</u>

As explained in our introduction to base-12 numerology in chapter 2, every num-ber has a specific vibrational frequency that corresponds to certain characteristics and personality traits and, like everything, has both positive and negative potential. This applies to any single-digit number you may come across from 1 to <u>11</u> or any double-digit master number, such as 11, 22, or 33.

The energetic personality of each of the single-digit numbers is summarized in table 8, including its positive attributes and negative tendencies.

Number	Meaning	Positive Attributes	Negative Tendencies
0	Potential	Optimistic, hopeful, enthusiastic, empowered, unlimited	Apprehensive, indecisive, overwhelmed, intimidated
1	New Beginnings	Self-assured, independent, confident, driven, original, authoritative, accountable	Selfish, arrogant, aggressive, self-critical, fearful, isolated, vulnerable
2	Duality	Cooperative, peaceful, inclusive, social, balanced, objective	Competitive, adversarial, critical, judgmental, defensive, moody
3	Catalyst	Influential, motivational, supportive, creative, eloquent	Manipulative, opinionated, pushy, meddling, deceptive
4	Structure	Stable, secure, organized, dependable, logical, practical, realistic	Inflexible, stubborn, cautious, private, perfectionist, unrealistic
5	Change	Active, energetic, adaptable, adventurous, spontaneous, courageous	Restless, impatient, unpredictable, irresponsible, reckless

Number	Meaning	Positive Attributes	Negative Tendencies
6	Love	Harmonious, compassionate, caring, supportive, accepting	Self-sacrificing, doting, meddling, over-sensitive, needy
7	Truth	Knowledgeable, authentic, purposeful, devout, spiritual	Pretentious, over-analytical, skeptical, preachy, fanatical, elitist
8	Manifesta-tion	Abundant, productive, practical, physically/spiritually balanced, grateful	Lacking, materialistic, entitled, ambitious, extravagant, wasteful
9	Completion	Fulfilled, content, accepting, forgiving, humanitarian, selfless, dedicated	Unfulfilled, defeated, vengeful, regretful, fatalistic, relentless
<u>10</u>	Awareness	Insightful, intuitive, perceptive, open minded, curious, focused	Distracted, confused, prying, paranoid, selective, obsessive
<u>11</u>	Illumination	Understanding, knowing, wise, receptive, inspired	Oblivious, unreceptive, naïve, disillusioned, ignorant

Table 8. The Meaning of the Single-Digit Numbers

Examples: How to Apply the Number Meanings

Let's continue our earlier example of the words *nature* and *business* to see how we apply these meanings to the numbers we came up with.

We determined that the letter energies of the word *nature* give a total of $5 + 1 + 2 + 3 + 9 + 5 = 25$ in base-10, which converts to $2 \times 12 + 1 = 21$ in base-12 and reduces to a single-digit energy of $2 + 1 = 3$, denoted 21/3. Using table 8 above, we can look up the meaning for 21/3 to see that *nature* means catalyst (3) through the duality (2) of new beginnings (1). This would seem a very accurate characterization of nature, as a catalyst of creativity (3) through the cooperation and balance (2) of new life (1).

Just as every number energy has both positive and negative characteristics, every word does too. The word *nature* resonates with not only the more positive meaning above, but also a harsher side: nature as the catalyst for adaptation (3) through the life and death duality (2) of survival of the fittest (1).

We likewise determined that the letter energies of the word *business* sum to $2 + 3 + 1 + 9 + 5 + 5 + 1 + 1 = 27$ in base-10, which converts to 2x12 + 3 = 23 in base-12 and reduces to 2 + 3 = 5 or 23/5. Looking up the meaning for 23/5, we find that *business* means change (5) through the duality (2) of the catalyst (3). Again, a fitting interpretation in that business is all about the transformation of resources into goods and services (5) by balancing supply with demand (2) of the market as catalyst for that demand (3).

Still, the 23/5 vibration of the word *business* also resonates with a meaning of maximizing profit and growth (5) through competitive (2) marketing pressure (3). This reflects the polarized potential of business as a force for both positive and negative change; positive in the form of employment and the creation of goods and services needed by society, as well as negative in the form of materialism, greed, and environmental neglect. Interestingly, the word *money* has the same 23/5 vibration of *business* (money = $4 + 6 + 5 + 5 + 7 = 2x12 + 3 = 23/5$).

The Masculine-Feminine Balance

One further quality about number energies that is useful to know is that every number has either a masculine (odd number) bias or feminine (even number) bias which work together to maintain neutral balance across the base-12 cycle. Note that these masculine and feminine biases are not in the context of gender but simply a way of describing contrasting energies.

All the odd-number energies of 1, 3, 5, 7, 9, and <u>11</u> are considered masculine as they are dynamic influences that call us to action: a new beginning occurs (1), a catalytic event is encountered (3), a change happens (5), a spiritual truth is revealed (7), an ending is reached (9), or a truth is illuminated (11). These tend to happen quickly as distinct events or sudden realizations, while their effects, the even number energies of 2, 4, 6, 8, and 10, are the more gradual and thoughtful "feminine" responses taken by us as we integrate the new reality. That is, we need time to work our way through the duality of relationships and polarized situations (2), we tend to dwell in places that feel safe and stable (4), we hold tightly onto love and harmony once found (6), we manifest gradually the legacies we build (8), and we need to pause for reflection and contemplation (10).

As the masculine and feminine energies alternate back and forth across the base-12 cycle, this helps us maintain a neutral perspective as we work our way through the experiences we encounter. It is only when we attempt to "jump a step" from masculine to masculine or feminine to feminine that we become imbalanced.

Examples of a Masculine Imbalance

Let's say, for example, you meet a new person (1) and start trying to push the relationship forward (3) without seeking to understand the other person or work together as a couple (2). This would lead to a very one-sided relationship in which you are overly asserting masculine themes and devaluing the other person.

Or perhaps you are in a long-term caring relationship with someone, but you're both having a bad day. You get into a heated argument over something trivial in which you both say hurtful things (3). Rather than taking some time to cool down and gather your thoughts (4), you break up on the spot out of anger (5). Here you jump from the 3 energy to the 5 and skip the 4, again resulting in a masculine imbalance.

Examples of a Feminine Imbalance

Now let's consider a couple of situations in which an overly feminine bias can be the cause of imbalance. Say you're in a stable and secure job (4) but one that doesn't inspire you at all. You get approached from another company to offer you your dream job in which you can pursue your passions (6), but you pass up the opportunity, too afraid to make the change (5). Here, you focused on the feminine energies of 4 and 6 without acting on the 5.

And one more example: After living a full and abundant life (8), your dear grandfather passes of natural causes (9). However, you are unable to reflect on the good times you had together and appreciate the wonderful life he had (10) because you haven't allowed yourself to properly grieve and find closure (9). In this instance, not honoring the masculine energy of the 9 made the transition from 8 to 10 a more difficult one.

It is this polarized nature of number vibrations, both in terms of positive/negative and masculine/feminine, that reminds us we are in control of our own destiny. How we react, feel, think or act in any situation is always our choice. Thus, the real power of numerology is that it shows us the full energetic potential in every experience so that we can make more positive and balanced choices. Because we are all tuned to the love-centered frequency of the 6, we are naturally drawn to do that anyway. This is our inner voice; that sense of conscience, integrity and right versus wrong that's always there in the background. Granted, we don't always choose to take the higher ground. But the more we do listen to our intuition, the more we will be compelled to make loving and responsible choices.

Still, the ability and desire to make a highly enlightened and selfless choice within any given situation requires a particularly elevated understanding of the number energy being experienced. This elevated understanding, or mastery, of number vibrations in numerology is where master numbers come in.

Special Case: The Master Numbers

A *master number* is a twin number such as 11, 22, or 33 and can be thought of as a higher octave of the single-digit number being repeated. As such, music is a great analogy for master numbers.

A higher octave of any note in the chromatic scale is a full cycle of twelve steps above the original note. So too with number energies: a higher octave of 1 is reached by completing a full cycle of 12 beyond the 1, or 1x12 + 1 = 11 in base-12. Thus, 11 is the master number of the 1 energy. As the 1 is all about new beginnings, independence, and self, master number 11 represents mastery of self. In practical terms, this means experiencing and understanding the 1 theme not only from the perspective of the 1 as a single-digit frequency but also from the higher perspective of the 1 as a full cycle of frequencies.

This same idea applies to the other ten master numbers from 22 to 11 11. Master number 22 requires an understanding of the theme of duality both as a frequency of 2 and as 2 cycles, whereas master number 33 involves knowing the 3 theme of the catalyst both as a frequency of 3 and from the higher perspective as 3 cycles.

Still, the high vibration of any master number is difficult to sustain for anyone other than a very spiritually evolved master. For the rest of us who are still walking the path toward mastery, we experience master numbers by alternating back and forth between two levels of intensity: their higher, unreduced double-digit master vibration and their calmer single-digit personality when reduced. As such, the more spiritually advanced we are, the longer we can hold the elevated master number vibrations and their higher selfless qualities.

For instance, when we are not able to maintain the innovative, inspirational, and idealistic intensity of the master number 11, we downshift to the $1 + 1 = 2$ of duality and its positive characteristics of cooperation, balance, and peace, but also its negative tendencies for conflict, competition, and judgment. So even master numbers aren't immune to the positive-negative polarity of our free will, particularly the lower master numbers.

Master Numbers Clarified in Base-12

In traditional base-10 numerology, only the first three master numbers of 11, 22, and 33 are typically considered. The conventional interpretations of these numbers are of 11 as illumination, 22 as the master builder, and 33 as the master healer/teacher. The reason given for these being the only valid master numbers in numerology is that humanity has only evolved spiritually to that level of understanding and enlightenment.

I would agree with this from the perspective of those rare individuals capable of sustaining that level of mastery constantly, such as the Buddha and Jesus, who embodied the 33 master catalyst qualities of profound teaching, healing, and love continuously. However, I believe all of us do experience moments of even higher mastery, however brief, that surpass the 33:

- We embody the 44 of mastery of structure whenever we provide order and stability for others in need, such as raising a child, caring for the elderly, or protecting the environment.

- We exemplify the 55 of mastery of change whenever we release fear and completely trust, such as when falling in love or going skydiving out of a perfectly good airplane!

- We embrace the 66 of mastery of love when we feel unconditional love for another, such as when a mother holds her newborn baby for the first time.

- We experience the 77 of mastery of truth when we receive a flash of absolute knowledge, such as when we intuitively know who is going to call just before the phone rings or we get an immediate gut feeling about a stranger we meet.

- We achieve the 88 of mastery of manifestation when feel absolute abundance, such as when we meet the person of our dreams or overcome a life-threatening illness.

- We arrive at the 99 of mastery of completion when we reach absolute acceptance, such as when we are in our final moments of physical life and ready to transition back to spirit.

- We realize the <u>10</u> <u>10</u> of mastery of awareness when we experience absolute awareness, such as when we communicate with spirit in a lucid dream, have a near-death experience, or transition and see our spiritual family waiting to greet us.

- Last, we attain the <u>11</u> <u>11</u> of mastery of illumination when we achieve absolute understanding. This I believe can only be reached when we return to spirit and reconnect with the full consciousness of our higher self.

As such, I acknowledge the appearance of any and all master numbers that appear in numerology readings. I don't believe we would have chosen a birth date or name that held a certain master number potential if we were just going to disregard it, assuming ourselves unworthy of at least aspiring toward it.

After all, mastery isn't a sudden accomplishment. It's a gradual process of learning more and more about a number theme over many lifetimes until that theme becomes second nature and a core strength. Until then, we strive to experience many moments of mastery as we hone that strength. And to do that, we need to place that master number energy somewhere within our personal numerology to draw those experiences toward us and to give us a skill set that enables us to work toward it.

Another issue in base-10 numerology that is cleared up in base-12 concerns the master number 11. In base-10, 11 is always treated as a double-digit master number meaning illumination because the base-10 cycle only goes from 0 to 9. In base-12, however, the <u>11</u> of illumination is not a double-digit number and therefore cannot be a master number. This means that the true master number 11, as consisting of 1 cycle of 12 plus 1, must have a distinct meaning of its own. As no meaning exists in traditional numerology for this, I had to derive one.

As each master number is meant to reflect the mastery of the number being doubled, the 11 should therefore mean the mastery of the 1 of the independent self, or mastery of self. This aligns well with the established meanings of the 22 as the master builder who has mastered duality (2) and the 33 as the master healer/teacher who has mastered the energy of being a catalyst for others (3).

A further discrepancy between base-10 and base-12 is that *all* master numbers in base-10 reduce to the single-digit <u>11</u> in base-12, as shown below. As such, any master number that shows up in a base-10 numerology reading is actually the vibration of illumination in base-12, not the higher level of mastery suggested.

Base-10		Base-12
11	=	**11**
22	=	1x12 + <u>10</u> = 1<u>10</u> = 1 + <u>10</u> = **11**
33	=	2x12 + 9 = 29 = 2 + 9 = **11**
44	=	3x12 + 8 = 38 = 3 + 8 = **11**
55	=	4x12 + 7 = 47 = 4 + 7 = **11**
66	=	5x12 + 6 = 56 = 5 + 6 = **11**
77	=	6x12 + 5 = 65 = 6 + 5 = **11**
88	=	7x12 + 4 = 74 = 7 + 4 = **11**
99	=	8x12 + 3 = 83 = 8 + 3 = **11**

Similarly, the base-10 numbers that *do* convert to master numbers in base-12 are overlooked as the master numbers they really are.

Base-10		Base-12
13 = 1 + 3 = 13/4	=	1x12 + 1 = **11**
26 = 2 + 6 = 26/8	=	2x12 + 2 = **22**
39 = 3 + 9 = 12/3	=	3x12 + 3 = **33**
52 = 5 + 2 = 52/7	=	4x12 + 4 = **44**
65 = 6 + 5 = 65/11	=	5x12 + 5 = **55**
78 = 7 + 8 = 15/6	=	6x12 + 6 = **66**
91 = 9 + 1 = 10/1	=	7x12 + 7 = **77**
104 = 1 + 0 + 4 = 104/5	=	8x12 + 8 = **88**
117 = 1 + 1 + 7 = 117/9	=	9x12 + 9 = **99**
130 = 1 + 3 + 0 = 130/4	=	<u>10</u>x12 + <u>10</u> = **<u>10</u> <u>10</u>**
143 = 1 + 4 + 3 = 143/8	=	<u>11</u>x12 + <u>11</u> = **<u>11</u> <u>11</u>**

Life Path Numbers Beyond Master 33 Are Rare

It's worth noting that master number life paths higher than 33 are mathematically less likely in personal numerology readings. This is because the sum of the reduced birth month, day, and year rarely exceed that. This applies to base-12 and base-10.

In base-12, for example, to have a master number 33 for a life path you would need a master 22 birth day (26 in base-10; see table 5 on page 37) and a combination of birth month and year that add to master 11 (13 in base-10) such as a 7 month (July) and a 6 year (2019; see table 6). However, that's as high as you can go *for now* because there's no combination of month and year that, when reduced in base-12, will give master 22 (26 in base-10). The maximum month is <u>11</u> (November) and you can't get the 15 as a reduced year that's needed to sum to a total of 26.

I say master number 33 is the highest life path we can get *for now* because a master 33 year does occur every once in a while, and when combined with a birth day and month that add to master 11 (13 in base-10), such as an 8 day and 5 month (May), one could conceivably have a master 44 life path. However, the last time that happened was in the year 39 (33 in base-12; see table 5) and the next will be in the year 12,095 (6 <u>11</u> <u>11</u> <u>11</u> in base-12, which reduces to 6 + <u>11</u> + <u>11</u> + <u>11</u> = 39 in base-10 = 3x12 + 3 = 33 in base-12). As that's pretty far off, let's not worry about a 44 life path for now.

Similarly, in base-10, to get a master number 33 for a life path you would need a master 22 birth day and a combination of birth month and year that add to master 11, such as 8 (August) + 3 (2019, since 2 + 0 + 1 + 9 = 12 = 1 + 2 = 3). However, that's the limit too *for now* because there's no combination of month and year in base-10 that will total 22 to add to your 22 day of birth for a 44 life path. The maximum reduced month or year you can have in base-10 is 9, so that rules out getting a 44 life path.

I suspect this is the actual underlying reason why traditional base-10 numerology doesn't venture beyond master number 33.

As with base-12, a master 33 year will roll around eventually, making a 44 life path possible in base-10 too. This occurred last in the year 33 and will do so again in the year 6999 (which reduces to 6 + 9 + 9 + 9 = 33). So again, don't wait up for a 44 life path.

Expression and Maturity Numbers beyond Master 33 Are More Common

When it comes to birth names, master numbers above 33 for Expression numbers are more possible in both base-12 and base-10. You just need a full name with lots of high-value letters that add to 44, 55, or a higher multiple of 11, or you need first, middle, and last names that are each master numbers themselves.

Perhaps the ancient practice of giving long and elaborate birth names to nobility was driven in part by numerology, or more accurately, the abuse of numerology. Many royal courts were known to have had numerologists and astrologists as advisers to the crown, so selecting names that resulted in master numbers gave the appearance of divine mastery. Still, had the child been named by its parents freely and intuitively without advisers "doing the math" of forcing a masterful name, their true nature would have been expressed more authentically.

In the case of maturity numbers, getting a master number above 33 is even more doable since the maturity number is calculated by adding together the life path and expression number. So, for example, if you have an 11 life path and a 33 expression number, you will have a 44 maturity number and likely a very busy adulthood happily helping everyone else achieve stability, order, and abundance.

Polarity Dissolves with Greater Mastery

With greater mastery comes greater selflessness and less tendency toward negative ego-based frailties. Again, the idea behind a master number is that it is a higher octave of the single-digit number being mastered. This means that the higher the master number, the more lower master number themes it also embodies.

The 22 of mastery of duality for instance has mastered not only the idealistic visionary qualities of the 11 of mastery of self but also the physical-spiritual balance of the 22 needed to apply that vision in practical ways. Likewise, the 33 of the master catalyst has similarly achieved the qualities of the 11 and 22 in order to teach those qualities to others.

At the 66 of mastery of love, we encounter a special state of being where the idea of vibrational polarity no longer applies—the singularity of love at the very heart of the base-12 numerology cycle. Here we gain the enlightened neutral perspective that polarity is simply vibrational balance for the greater good. Polarity therefore loses its positive/negative connotation of good versus bad and becomes one of vibrational fullness instead.

It is from this benevolent and non-judgmental vantage of the master 66 that the higher master numbers can see, though still subject to the vibrational polarity of the human experience.

What the Double-Digit Master Numbers Mean from 11 to <u>11 11</u>

Summarized in table 9 below are the eleven master numbers of base-12 numerology, including the traditional meanings for 22 and 33 and my interpretations of 11 and 44 through <u>11 11</u>. Also shown are the lower octave single-digit vibration each master number reduces to when not being expressed fully and, to the right, the master number's negative tendencies, if any.

Master Number	Meaning	Positive Attributes	Negative Tendencies
11	Mastery of Self	Authentic, idealistic visionary, self-aware, honest, consistent Downshifts to $1 + 1 = 2$ of **duality**	2: Competitive, critical, adversarial, judgmental, defensive, moody
22	Mastery of Duality	Master builder, practical visionary, generous, physical-spiritual balance Downshifts to $2 + 2 = 4$ of **structure and stability**	4: Inflexible, stubborn, cautious, perfectionist, private, unrealistic
33	Master Catalyst	Master healer/teacher, catalyst of compassion Downshifts to $3 + 3 = 6$ of **love and harmony**	6: Self-sacrificing, doting, meddling, needy, over-sensitive
44	Mastery of Structure	Master engineer, facilitator of order and stability downshifts to $4 + 4 = 8$ of **manifestation**	8: Lacking, entitled, materialistic, ambitious, extravagant, wasteful

Master Number	Meaning	Positive Attributes	Negative Tendencies
55	Mastery of Change	Master of change and growth, absolute allowance, and trust Downshifts to 5 + 5 = <u>**10**</u> of **awareness**	<u>10</u>: Distracted, prying, confused, paranoid, selective, obsessive
66	Mastery of Love	Unconditional love Downshifts to 6 + 6 = 1x12 + 0 = 10/**1** of **new beginnings**	1: Selfish, arrogant, aggressive, self-critical, fearful, isolated, vulnerable
77	Mastery of Truth	Absolute knowledge Downshifts to 7 + 7= 1x12 + 2 = 12/**3** of the **catalyst**	3: Manipulative, opinionated, pushy, meddling, deceptive
88	Mastery of Manifestation	Absolute abundance Downshifts to 8 + 8 = 16 = 1x12 + 4 = 14/**5** of **change**	5: Restless, impatient, reactionary, domineering
99	Mastery of Completion	Absolute acceptance Downshifts to 9 + 9 = 1x12 + 6 = 16/**7** of **spiritual truth**	7: Pretentious, over-analytical, skeptical, preachy, fanatical, elitist
<u>**10 10**</u>	Mastery of Awareness	Absolute awareness Downshifts to <u>10</u> + <u>10</u> = 1x12 + 8 = 18/**9** of **completion**	9: Unfulfilled, defeated, vengeful, regretful, fatalistic
<u>**11 11**</u>	Mastery of Illumination	Absolute understanding Downshifts to <u>11</u> + <u>11</u> = 1x12 + <u>10</u> = 1<u>10</u>/<u>**11**</u> of **illumination**	<u>11</u>: Oblivious, unreceptive, naïve, disillusioned, ignorant

Table 9. The Meaning of the Double-Digit Master Numbers

Examples: How to Apply the Master Number Meanings

To get a feel for how master numbers work, let's consider an example of a well-known figure whose numerology includes a master number, United States president Donald Trump.

Based on the letters of Donald's full birth name, Donald John Trump, his expression number is the master number 11. This is obtained by first looking up the number energies for all the individual letters in his birth name using table 1 (page 30), adding the numbers together for each of his three names and reducing to single digits, then adding together those three single digits and reducing as required to get a final single digit.

Donald John Trump = (4 + 6 + 5 + 1 + 3 + 4) + (1 + 6 + 8 + 5) + (2 + 9 + 3 + 4 + 7)

$$= (1x12 + \underline{11}) + (1x12 + 8) + (2x12 + 1)$$
$$= \underline{111} + 18 + 21 = (1 + \underline{11}) + (1 + 8) + (2 + 1)$$
$$= (1x12 + 0) + 9 + 3 = 10 + 9 + 3 = (1 + 0) + 9 + 3$$
$$= 1 + 9 + 3 = 1x12 + 1 = \text{master } 11$$

Recall that a person's expression number indicates how they express themselves—what their general direction in life will be and the particular talents, traits, and preferences they were born with to pursue their life path.

Donald's expression number of master 11 indicates his persona and focus is all about self-mastery at best and competitiveness and conflict at worst. We see this clearly, both in his strong self-confidence and resilience and his aggressive personal style, confrontational business approach, and need to get his way. He is the quintessential deal maker. Not surprisingly, the numerology of the word *deal* itself matches the master 11 vibration of his Expression number (deal = 4 + 5 + 1 + 3 = 1x12 + 1 = master 11).

We also see that when he's not running at the full throttle of his 11 master number, he downshifts to the calmer, more cooperative, and socially engaging vibe of the 1 + 1 = 2 of duality, relationships, and balance. This makes him a classic example of a master number being expressed through its full range of potential.

Let's take a look at another example of a master number, this time as expressed through the word *carbon*, the element upon which all organic life on earth is built. Using table 1, we obtain the following:

carbon = 3 + 1 + 9 + 2 + 6 + 5

      = 26 in base-10

      = 2x12 + 2 in base-12 = master 22

We see that the base-12 numerology of carbon is fittingly the 22 of mastery of duality, the master builder, perfectly matching its role as a building block of life.

Now one final example with the word *gravity*, a fundamental force of nature that enables matter to form and life to exist. Referring to table 1 once more, we look up the number energy of each letter and then add and reduce to a single digit.

gravity = 7 + 9 + 1 + 4 + 9 + 2 + 7

      = 39 in base-10

      = 3x12 + 3 in base-12 = master 33

Master number 33 is the master catalyst and a fitting vibrational meaning for gravity as a universal catalyst for physical reality.

Putting It All Together: The Base-12 Numerology Cycle

Before we get into the meaning of each number in detail, we need to understand how they all work together. Numbers, like people, never operate in total isolation and it is their relationship to each other through the base-12 numerology cycle that gives them meaning.

As mentioned in the introduction, the meaning of each number is described by its position in the base-12 cycle (see figure 2 below). The dashed and black waves reflect the vibrational boundaries of our reality, and the infinity-shaped area they contain is our playing field of potential. Likewise, the changing gap between the two waves as we progress from one number's energy to the next, and its positive/negative polarity relative to the neutral axis, characterizes the vibrational personality of each number.

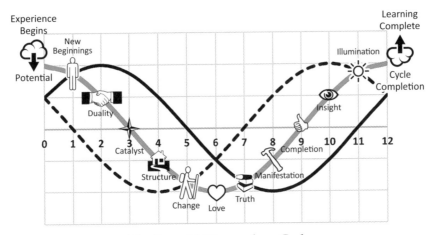

The Base-12 Numerology Cycle

A beautiful thing about this pattern is that it is universal in scope. It portrays not only each experience we encounter as a full vibrational cycle from the 0 of potential through the <u>11</u> of illumination, but also each cycle of physical incarnation from birth to our return to spirit. Let's walk through the full number cycle to appreciate this better.

0	Every experience starts from the 0 of *potential* and unlimited possibility.
1	We step into that experience at 1 as a *new beginning*, feeling the independence, exposure, and separation that brings.
2	As we engage the situation at 2, we experience the *duality* and contrast this new relationship involves.
3	From the polarized push and pull of the 2, we reach the *catalyst* of the 3, which urges us to take action one way or another to deal with the duality.
4	This urge is naturally toward the *structure*, stability, and safety of the 4.
5	Eventually becoming restless, we seek the freedom and *change* of the 5.

6	This frees us from our fears enough to take a leap of faith toward the 6 of *love*.
7	Having found the joy and harmony that only love can provide, we reach beyond our ego to *truth* and higher knowledge.
8	With knowledge and belief comes the confidence to *manifest abundance* of the 8 and, when spiritually motivated, selflessly for the greater good.
9	Having manifested our vison into reality, we reach the *completion* of the 9.
<u>10</u>	From completion and closure comes the greater *awareness* of the insightful <u>10</u>.
<u>11</u>	Through awareness, we can see the lessons *illuminated* by the <u>11</u>, bringing this understanding with us as we return to the 0 of potential to begin the next cycle.

The Path of Resonance

We just saw how the various number energies of base-12 numerology flow together as a logical cycle and how each energy helps prepare us for the next. Still, how do we apply this powerful knowledge effectively in the hustle and bustle of our daily lives?

To live a full and authentic life is to resonate with the base-12 cycle of nature. This means striving to match the natural state of that vibrational blueprint in our thoughts, feelings and actions as we encounter each of the twelve energies. Every energy as discussed has its own unique vibrational profile, a window of opportunity within which we can choose how to respond. And each energy, other than the pure singularity energies of the 6 of love and 0 of potential, offer a range of response.

Thus, to resonate fully with any number's vibration means experiencing its full range of potential. Yet that's impossible as we can only choose one response at a time.

Here's the good news. Since the base-12 vibrational cycle consists of two overlapping waves, adding them together reveals the net vibration that would result if you *could* experience their entire range at once. If you recall, that net vibration is the gray overall wave. So, to follow the path of the gray overall curve is to follow your most resonant path.

With that insight, let's revisit each of the twelve energies once more to understand in practical terms what "following the gray curve" really means. For each energy, I will describe what its upper and lower expressions vibrationally represent and what the gray curve suggests is our most balanced strategy for achieving resonance.

Note that the vibrational strategy I offer below is by no means a narrow and restrictive recipe that everyone must follow to live a fulfilling and happy life. It's simply the natural vibrational pattern to which we already resonate when we allow ourselves to. What these recommendations provide are general guidelines to help you recognize when you are out of tune with some aspect of your authentic vibration and how to get back into tune.

There are unlimited ways in which we can each achieve and maintain resonance with that love-centred essence of who we are in our own unique and creative way. That's what free choice is all about. Still, it's nice to know that our free choice always has a subtle vibrational bias, a divine flow perpetually nudging and guiding us toward the love, compassion and harmony of the 6.

0

The 0 has special meaning as emphasized throughout this book. Rather than a specific vibration like the other eleven, it represents the *potential* of *all* number vibrations from 0 to 11 and of *all* letter vibrations from A to Z.

Like the 6 of love, the 0 is a singularity created by the intersection of the two prime waves. Because it is a singularity with no "gap" between the two waves, it possesses no polarity or duality. It is the pure state of potential just as the 6 is the pure state of harmony we call love. Unlike the 6, however, the 0 marks both the end of one cycle and the beginning of the next. It therefore represents the unlimited potential of each cycle of experience *and* the completion of all infinite possible outcomes simultaneously.

This reveals the paradoxical timelessness of consciousness, where past and future are only illusions of the infinite now. Also, where the gray curve at 6 calls for complete allowance and surrender (maximum amplitude below the neutral axis), the 0 calls for the opposite (with the gray wave at its maximum above). This encourages us to approach each new experience with positivity, optimism, and confidence. Again, we attract what we vibrationally believe. As above, so below.

1

The 1 energy resonates with the vibration of new beginnings, originality, and leadership at its highest level (upper black wave) and with isolation, ego, and fear at its lowest level (lower dashed wave).

The gray combined wave at 1 tells us that our most natural response is to choose the highest response as described above, as both the upper black wave and gray overall wave fall on the same point. This follows from the fact that the lowest response falls on the neutral axis itself, meaning fear and ego often immobilizes us through caution or stubbornness and makes zero contribution to a positive vibration overall.

As 1 is the first energy we encounter in all new situations (birth, new relationship, new job, new skill, new project, new day, new conversation, etc.), it determines our initial trajectory into the learning cycle and how strong a start we make. Thus, when beginning anything new, it's beneficial to hold as positive and enthusiastic an attitude as possible and keep your ego out of it. This also explains why rising above our ego and fear are two of the biggest challenges we face; they surface most strongly in the very circumstances that are new and unfamiliar to us. As such, a weak and fearful response to the 1 energy severely limits what we can experience going forward.

2

The 2 is the energy of duality or polarity. In its highest expression, it represents cooperation, balance, and peace (upper black wave), and in it lowest, conflict, judgment and resistance (lower dashed wave).

The gray overall wave for 2 indicates that greatest resonance is not achieved at its highest expression of cooperation as one might expect, but halfway between the highest and neutrality. This indicates that, although we should always seek cooperative win-win outcomes, we also need to avoid giving away our personal power or suppressing our opinions for the sake of avoiding confrontation. An important message here as it shows that speaking our truth and standing up for what we believe, even if unpopular, is a key element of living an authentic life. And as many of us have experienced, suppressing our voice only leads to inner stress that eventually manifests in unhealthy ways.

Also, just as how positively we exited the 1 energy determined our vibrational entry point into 2, how we handle 2 sets our angle of approach into 3. Again, how we experience each situation sets the tone for the next.

3

The 3 is the catalytic energy. The definition of a catalyst is that which causes change without changing itself. As such, the 3 is the fight-or-flight instinct we feel when unforeseen events or situations occur and prompt us to act. The highest response to the catalyst is to use the experience constructively to bring about positive change (upper black wave), while the lowest is to see it only as negative, feel defeated by it, and play the victim.

For the 3, we see that the gray overall wave reflects the neutral unbiased energy of the catalyst itself. Thus, the 3 calls for the neutral objectivity of understanding the situation fully in order make an informed response rather than an emotionally biased one. As neutral objectivity can appear and feel vibrationally the same as not responding at all, it's all too easy to fall into the rut of putting your head in the sand and waiting for the storm to pass. As such, whenever you feel a neutral response is in order, do a quick gut-check to confirm if your inaction is well considered or actually avoidance out of fear.

I find it interesting too that the 3 (and its enlightened counterpart the 9) possesses the maximum vibrational range or amplitude of the entire base-12 cycle. This makes catalytic situations very powerful opportunities to make major course corrections in your life when necessary. So, the key is to see them as helpful detours guiding you to a better route rather than as dead ends spoiling the trip.

4

The 4 is the energy of structure. At its highest level, the 4 resonates with stability, order and predictability, and at its lowest, with instability, disorder and insecurity. The 4 energy is our natural yearning for stability and calm after the dynamic and often disruptive 3 of the catalyst. It helps us vibrationally take a time-out and adjust to the new direction and find our bearings.

The overall gray wave reveals a balance point for the 4 to be halfway down below the neutral axis. This indicates that our most beneficial response to the 4 is to lean toward less structure and rigidity rather than more, while still ensuring sufficient order to feel safe. This is consistent with the principle of the law of attraction, whereby we will manifest more effectively by detaching from specific expectations and allowing the universe freedom to provide the best outcome for the greatest good.

5

Where the 3 is the energy of causing change, the 5 is the energy of change itself. Its highest expression is that of movement, action, and drive, of pushing for change, while its lowest expression is of momentum, allowance, and trust, of going with the flow of change.

The overall gray wave shows that our most natural resonance with the 5 vibration is of near complete allowance and trust, with the gray wave intersecting the lower dashed prime wave. This means that we need to trust our intuition deeply and allow synchronicity to guide us forward, rather than impatiently forcing things. Through patience and trust, we can enjoy the present moment more while allowing the universe to bring us more opportunities to explore. Conversely, when we try to accelerate life and perpetually yearn for more, all we're doing is projecting a vibration of discontent and lack. This in turn just manifests more unfulfilling experiences because that's precisely what our vibrational belief is asking for.

6

The 6 is the all-important frequency of love. It represents a singularity, a point of timelessness where the two prime waves intersect. As such, there is no higher or lower level to authentic love, only a state of being that is already complete in and of itself.

As at 0, the gray path of resonance at 6 achieves the maximum amplitude possible but does so below the neutral axis instead of above. Thus, where 0 represents our unlimited potential in the spiritual plane, the 6 of love is our full potential in the physical plane. This suggests we must completely allow, trust, and surrender to love to fully experience it. We literally need to let ourselves energetically "fall" in love. And if we approach the 6 of love from the flexible trajectory of trust and allowance instilled in 5, that fall is a natural one.

7

The 7 represents truth and knowledge and is the enlightened place at which we first arrive when we step through the doorway of love. The gray wave of the 7 is the same as that of the 5 of change, of allowance and going with the flow of our intuition. The 7, however, puts us on an upward trajectory to rise to ever higher levels of awareness.

8

The 8 is the energy of manifestation and abundance, the spiritually confident counterpart to the cautious and responsible 4 of structure and stability. As such, the 8 and the 4 both share the same gray wave position, biased halfway below the neutral axis toward greater allowance and flexibility more than tighter control and authority. Where the 4 places our focus on personal abundance, however, the 8 expands our view to serving the greater good.

9

The 9 is the energy of completions and endings. Like its less aware counterpart, the 3 of the catalyst, the 9 calls for objectivity and neutrality as shown by the gray curve intersecting the neutral axis. Also like the 3, the 9 presents the greatest range of how we may respond. Unlike the 3, however, the 9 urges us to bring closure and acceptance to situations in order to move on rather than just changing direction as prompted by the catalytic 3.

10

The 10 is the vibration of awareness and insight, of the individual (1) seeing the full potential (0) in each experience and in ourselves. The gray wave at 10, being halfway above the neutral axis, calls for a positive bias of seeing the potential for good in all things and all people. Where its less enlightened counterpart, the 2 of duality, encourages cooperation and balance in relationships without sacrificing your personal power, the 10 broadens that mission for the greater good without sacrificing our collective power.

11

The 11 is the vibration of illumination, of truth revealed. The 11 is the enlightened counterpart of the 1 of new beginnings and independence. Both share the same elevated position of the gray wave, though the 11 is ascending while the 1 is descending. Also, like the 1, the lowest range of the 11 is on the neutral axis. This means that we either recognize a truth being illuminated or we don't. In other words, what causes an "aha!" moment for one person can be entirely missed by another. It all depends on our individual level of awareness and willingness to see beyond our current comfort zone.

––––––

Although the path of resonance we have just discussed is the path of least resistance through the full cycle of twelve energies, you will find certain energies easier or harder to align than others. This is because you chose specific lessons to explore in this life. And to learn those lessons, you also chose life circumstances and personality traits that will draw you off the ideal path in those particular areas so that you can to find your way back through free choice.

In other words, you came into this life with an overall vibration that doesn't quite follow the path of resonance. You began with a slightly distorted personal vibe that reflects your soul's unique evolution as a divine work in progress. And to ensure you work on the right areas, you intentionally chose a birth date, a name, parents, and circumstances that would provide many opportunities to explore those particular themes. Isn't it reassuring to know that we are all perfectly flawed for a reason and that our greatest challenges are blessings in disguise?

Also, as we are all part of the same collective consciousness, the specific lessons and circumstances we choose are designed not only for our own soul's spiritual progression but also for the greater good of all. As such, our chosen role may be a personally difficult one that serves as a catalyst for the growth of others. This would include such things as choosing an illness, disability, or early death for yourself if that is what was deemed necessary to help family and friends explore their own chosen lessons.

I suspect we each take turns in this capacity within our soul group to help share these more difficult roles from one incarnation to the next. Still, our higher self always knows the overall plan and what our specific role is to be. We just need to follow the voice of our intuition about what excites us most as this will always keep us on our intended path.

The Number Meanings in Detail

Where the first half of the book enabled you to understand your vibrational profile in broad strokes, the second half provides all the information you need to understand each number in depth. A section is dedicated to each of the numbers from 0 to 11 as well as the master numbers from 11 to 11 11.

Each section begins with a description of the overall personality of the number and its range of expression, including its positive and negative qualities. This is followed by the specific meanings of the number as a final single-digit energy (outer energy), as well as the various two-digit combinations (inner influences) that can sum to give that final single-digit energy. For example, the 5 outer energy can appear on its own or through the following combinations of inner influences: 14/5, 41/5, 23/5, 32/5, and 50/5.

0 · Potential

Positive Qualities: Optimistic, hopeful, enthusiastic, empowered, unlimited

Negative Tendencies: Apprehensive, indecisive, overwhelmed, intimidated

Overall Personality of the 0

At its higher expression, the 0 is full of possibility, optimism, and hope, and at its lowest, it is indecisive, directionless, and intimidating. The infinite possibilities of the 0 can feel overwhelming at times, but following your intuition and your greatest joy will always guide you forward. Like the circle it represents, the 0 reminds us that everything and everyone is connected and that everything we do makes a difference.

What It Means When a 0 Appears

The 0 is unique in base-12 numerology as it never appears on its own in a numerology reading but rather alongside other numbers before final reduction, such as 10/1, 30/3, or 1203/6. By its very nature as a potential rather than a specific frequency, the 0 serves to modify the vibration of other numbers in terms of their potential. For example, where 1 represents new beginnings, 10 represents new beginnings (1) of potential (0).

1 · New Beginnings

Positive Qualities: Self-assured, independent, confident, driven, original, accountable, authoritative

Negative Tendencies: Selfish, arrogant, aggressive, self-critical, fearful, isolated, vulnerable

Overall Personality of the 1 Vibration

Standing tall and on its own, the 1 is the energy of new beginnings, independence, and self. It is our energetic introduction to the physical world at birth and our drive to survive and succeed as individuals. It has a personality of originality, initiative and leadership.

Preferring to be in charge, the 1 doesn't like to be controlled or told what to do. At its best, it is confident, enthusiastic, and inspiring, and at its worst, selfish, arrogant, and domineering. Though usually comfortable in public and the limelight, the 1 can feel defensive, isolated, and alone. An unresolved fear of failure often lurks behind the self-assured façade of the 1. It is from this sense of separateness that the 1 yearns for the connection and contrast of the 2.

What It Means When a 1 Appears as ...

1—Innovative Pioneer

When the 1 appears on its own, not from the reduction of the two-digit number 10/1, it projects the outer character of the 1 directly rather than in a roundabout way. This is an energy of new beginnings, independence, initiative, leadership, and originality. The 1 is also prone to its lower tendencies of being self-absorbed, aggressive, and tough on itself. At its highest vibration, the 1 is a confident, driven, and innovative leader, and at its lowest, an arrogant and pushy egomaniac that controls and intimidates others to get attention. 1s are often good starters and eager innovators but easily bored implementers and poor finishers.

10/1—Empowering Leader

When the 1 appears from the sum of 1 and 0, it projects the outer character of new beginnings through the inner influences of new beginnings (1) of potential (0). This means an energy of 1 through personal empowerment, freedom, and optimism. At its highest vibration, the 10/1 is an optimistic, inspiring, and empowering leader, and at its lowest a pessimistic, bossy, and critical lone wolf.

2 · Duality

Positive Qualities: Cooperative, peaceful, inclusive, social, balanced, objective

Negative Tendencies: Competitive, adversarial, critical, judgmental, defensive, moody

Overall Personality of the 2 Vibration

From the independence and new beginnings of the 1, we take our next step into the duality and polarity of 2. A powerful paradox is the 2, able to pull together or push apart at a moment's notice. Such is the split-personality of this temperamental number—clarity through contrast, compromise through opposition, acceptance through differences, spiritual growth through physical experience.

Polarized like a magnet, the energy of the 2 can either attract or repel, but always intensifies as others draw near. Prone to overreaction, the 2 can distort anxiety into defensiveness, attraction into obsession, diversity into bigotry, and disagreement into hatred. The 2 also has difficulty setting boundaries, walking the fine line between cooperation and conformance. The energy of both warrior and diplomat, the 2 is the double-edged sword of relationships, stalemates, and repeated patterns. As such, it often requires the catalytic force of the 3 to shake things loose.

What It Means When a 2 Appears as . . .

2—Team Player

When the 2 appears on its own, not from the reduction of a two-digit number, it projects the outer character of the 2 directly rather than in a roundabout way. This is an energy of duality, contrast, relationships, and finding balance. At its higher vibration the 2 is a friendly, considerate, and objective team player, and at its lower, uncooperative, difficult, and judgmental, playing the victim and seeking validation from others. 2s can be quite unpredictable and polarized, swinging back and forth between extremes of allowance and resistance. They can appear peaceful and together on the outside though conflicted and disconnected inside.

11—Master of Self

See page 136 for the meaning of this master number.

20/2—Objective Negotiator

When the 2 appears from the sum of 2 and 0, it projects the outer character of duality (2) through the inner influences of the duality (2) of potential (0). This means an energy of 2 through seeing the contrast and possibilities in situations. At its higher vibration, the 20/2 is the effective negotiator: objective, fair, and a good judge of character. At its lower level, it is indecisive, submissive, and compromising to the point of feeling defeated.

3 · Catalyst

Positive Qualities: Influential, motivational, supportive, creative, eloquent

Negative Tendencies: Manipulative, opinionated, pushy, meddling, deceptive

Overall Personality of the 3 Vibration

To break free from the challenging polarity of the 2, we often need the push of the catalytic 3. The 3 is the change agent of the base-12 cycle, prompting action while remaining unchanged itself.

Often dramatic and sometimes traumatic, the 3 can appear as unexpected events, encounters, and situations that transform our worldview in some way and nudge us in a new direction. Finding the value and lesson in each 3 we face can be tough, requiring perspective and positivity to respond constructively instead of feeling defeated and a victim of circumstances. Many times, we also play the role of the catalyst for others. The 3 is an outgoing, creative energy with a gift for communication but can become pushy, opinionated, and a poor listener. Nevertheless, the 3 can be persistent in helping us break unproductive patterns. And the more intense the catalytic period we encounter, the more we yearn for the stability, safety, and predictability of the 4.

What It Means When a 3 Appears as ...

3—Change Agent

When the 3 appears on its own, not from the reduction of a two-digit number, it projects the outer character of the 3 directly rather than in a roundabout way. This is an energy of the catalyst, causing change without changing itself. This includes characteristics such as creativity, communication, and stimulating positive action. At its higher vibration, the 3 is the creative change agent that brings out the best in others, and at its lower, an opinionated and meddling busybody that doesn't respect personal boundaries and pushes people's buttons just to get a reaction. 3s are typically outgoing and the life of the party, but they often crave attention and can act out in dramatic ways to get it.

12/3—Creative Synthesizer

When the 3 appears from the sum of 1 and 2, it projects the outer character of the catalyst (3) through the inner influences of new beginnings (1) of duality (2). At its higher vibration, the 12/3 is the creative synthesizer able to bring ideas and people together in complementary ways. This includes a flair for design, organization, and promotion. At its lower, the 12/3 is a troublemaker that instigates conflict and drama, looking for fault in others.

21/3—Creative Problem-Solver

When the 3 appears from the sum of 2 and 1, it projects the outer character of the catalyst (3) through the inner influences of the duality (2) of new beginnings (1). At its higher vibration, the 21/3 is the creative problem-solver able to assess situations and problems objectively and identify innovative solutions. At its lower level, the 21/3 is a self-doubting pessimist that sees the negative in things and imposes their limiting views on others.

30/3—Motivational Teacher

When the 3 appears from the sum of 3 and 0, it projects the outer character of the catalyst (3) through the inner influences of the catalyst (3) of potential (0). At its higher vibration, the 30/3 is the inspirational teacher and motivator able to bring out the full creative potential in people and ideas. At its lower expression, the 30/3 is a manipulative and deceitful influence peddler that tries to maneuver things in its own favor.

4 · Structure and Stability

Positive Qualities: Stable, secure, organized, dependable, logical, practical, realistic

Negative Tendencies: Inflexible, stubborn, cautious, private, perfectionist, unrealistic

Overall Personality of the 4 Vibration

Like the sturdy legs of a table or the solid walls of a building, the 4 is the energy of structure, stability, and order. The 4 personifies practicality, dependability, and reserve and is the rock that others lean on and rely upon to get the job done.

Rarely taking risks, the 4 prefers the predictability and safety of the status quo, the comfort zone of what is, not what could be. As such, the 4 is prone to inflexibility, caution, and stubbornness and is where complacency and conformance often take refuge under the guise of responsibility and duty. Still, we can only remain content with the predictability and stability of the 4 for so long. At some point, we yearn for the freedom and adventure of the 5.

What It Means When a 4 Appears as . . .

4—Dedicated Worker

When the 4 appears on its own, not from the reduction of a two-digit number, it projects the outer character of the 4 directly rather than in a roundabout way. This is the energy of structure and stability. At its higher vibration, the 4 embodies the steadfast characteristics of the dedicated worker: reliable, responsible, and practical; the solid pillar of the community and the first to lend a hand. The 4 is also prone to its lower tendencies of being reserved, cautious, inflexible, and stubborn. Not one to rock the boat or take risks, 4s tend to mind their own business and take the safe route. They can be quite private and cool, keeping their emotions hidden inside.

13/4—Restructuring Expert

When the 4 appears from the sum of 1 and 3, it projects the outer character of structure and stability (4) through the inner influences of new beginnings (1) of the catalyst (3). At its higher vibration, the 13/4 is the restructuring expert with a knack for creating order out of chaos and sense out of confusion. Excellent at recognizing patterns beneath the surface, the 13/4 is adept at simplifying systems and finding the easier way. At its lower level, the 13/4 is an overly cautious worrier that fears change and over-analyzes everything. Although attracting many opportunities for creative expression, it can be too risk-averse to pursue them.

31/4—Creative Architect

When the 4 appears from the sum of 3 and 1, it projects the outer character of structure and stability (4) through the inner influences of the catalyst (3) of new beginnings (1). At its higher vibration, the 31/4 is the creative architect of designing new structures and systems and catalyst for turning ideas into reality. At its lower level, the 31/4 is the rigid perfectionist that is hard to please, frequently dissatisfied with the work of others, and redoing things on its own. Obsessed with having things a certain way, it can stifle team work and stall progress.

22—Master of Duality

See page 137 for the meaning of this master number.

40/4—Shrewd Strategist

When the 4 appears from the sum of 4 and 0, it projects the outer character of structure and stability (4) through the inner influences of the structure and stability (4) of potential (0). At its highest vibration, the 40/4 is the shrewd planner and strategist, able to develop plans and scenarios that maximize their potential. At its lower expression, the 40/4 is the relentless drill sergeant that demands structure and order above all else and expects everyone and everything to comply to the same rigid standard.

5 · Change

Positive Qualities: Active, energetic, adaptable, adventurous, spontaneous, courageous

Negative Tendencies: Restless, impatient, unpredictable, irresponsible, reckless

Overall Personality of the 5 Vibration

The energy of the 5 is all about change and movement, the thrill seeker and restless traveler of the base-12 cycle.

Unlike the often unexpected 3 of the catalyst, the 5 is change we initiate. It may be the result of some catalyst we experience, but nevertheless is the subsequent action we choose. The 5 is our desire for something more, for expanding our senses and experiencing life more fully. As such, the 5 can stray into self-gratification, unpredictability, and irresponsibility. Still, the 5 is witty, unconventional, and always fun to be around. A trademark of the positive 5 is that it is trusting, fearless, and willing to explore the unknown. This enables the 5 to take the courageous journey toward the 6 of love and harmony, the most worthwhile destination of all.

What It Means When a 5 Appears as ...

5—Adaptable Adventurer

When the 5 appears on its own, not from the reduction of a two-digit number, it projects the outer character of the 5 directly rather than in a roundabout way. This is the energy of change, freedom, and trust. The 5 is the adaptable adventurer, eager to try new things, and take a chance. However, the 5 gets easily bored with routine and restless for stimulation. At its higher vibration, the 5 is the energetic, spontaneous, and courageous trend-setter willing to go first and blaze a trail. At its lowest level, the 5 is impatient, unpredictable, irresponsible, and unreliable, an adrenaline junky that never sits still and has contempt for rules and structure.

14/5—Custom Builder

When the 5 appears from the sum of 1 and 4, it projects the outer character of change (5) through the inner influences of new beginnings (1) of structure (4). At its higher vibration, the 14/5 is the custom builder with a talent for creating things of lasting value provided there's enough variety to keep it interesting. Resilient and adaptable, the 14/5 is able to bounce back from setbacks and call anyplace home. At its lower expression, the 14/5 is the transient wanderer unable to stick with commitments for any length of time. Easily distracted and bored, it is quick to move on in search of greener pastures.

41/5—Start-Up Specialist

When the 5 appears from the sum of 4 and 1, it projects the outer character of change (5) through the inner influences of structure (4) of new beginnings (1). At its higher vibration, the 41/5 is the start-up specialist able to coordinate new ventures and establish structure in a dynamic landscape. Organized and practical, the 41/5 takes life in stride and adapts to new situations calmly and methodically. At its lower expression, the 41/5 is insecure and homesick, torn between setting down roots and its restless nature.

23/5—Campaign Strategist

When the 5 appears from the sum of 2 and 3, it projects the outer character of change (5) through the inner influences of duality (2) of the catalyst (3). At its highest vibration, the 23/5 is the campaign strategist that understands what makes people tick and how to sway opinion. At its lowest level, the 23/5 can be very manipulative and deceitful and has no problem attacking the reputation of others just to get a reaction.

32/5—Crisis Manager

When the 5 appears from the sum of 3 and 2, it projects the outer character of change (5) through the inner influences of the catalyst (3) of duality (2). At its highest vibration, the 32/5 is the crisis manager, able to achieve balance and peace in the face of change. One who thrives in dynamic situations, the 32/5 is an expert at crisis prevention and damage control. At its lowest, the 32/5 is the devious troublemaker that enjoys instigating conflict and unrest.

50/5—Turnaround Specialist

When the 5 appears from the sum of 5 and 0, it projects the outer character of change (5) through the inner influences of change (5) of potential (0). At its highest vibration, the 50/5 is the turnaround specialist able to get things back on track and salvage unrealized potential. At its lowest, the 50/5 is unpredictable and inconsistent, unable to make up its mind and constantly changing direction.

6 · Love

Positive Qualities: Harmonious, compassionate, caring, supportive, accepting

Negative Tendencies: Self-sacrificing, doting, meddling, oversensitive, needy

Overall Personality of the 6 Vibration

We reach the midway point of our journey at the 6, the vibration of love. This is the very heart of the base-12 numerology cycle and the fulcrum upon which everything balances. The 6 represents the turning point of awareness in our physical-spiritual duality, and it is often at our lowest point that we finally discover the true meaning of love.

How deeply we experience the 6 and how openly we are willing to share our love with others depends on how much we first love ourselves. Without that self-worth, the 6 can be an emotional cup half empty of unhealthy relationships, neediness, self-sacrifice, and suffering. But, like the intersection point at the center of the infinity symbol, the 6 is a magical place where polarity can instantaneously reverse and propel us upward. And once we are on a positive trajectory powered by love, we are on our way to the spiritual truth of 7.

What It Means When a 6 Appears as ...
6—Compassionate Caregiver

When the 6 appears on its own, not from the reduction of a two-digit number, it projects the outer character of the 6 directly rather than in a roundabout way. This is the energy of love and harmony. At its higher vibration, the 6 is the compassionate caregiver. Loving and kind, the 6 is always willing to help others and create harmony wherever they go. Family and friends are extremely important to the 6. In its lower form, the 6 can stray to the extremes of self-sacrifice, neediness, and suffering. Sensitive by nature, the 6 often takes on the emotions of others and takes things personally. The 6 also tends to meddle in the personal lives of others, not realizing their desire to be helpful can be excessive. 6s often give generously to others but resist receiving help for themselves.

15/6—Ambassador of Love

When the 6 appears from the sum of 1 and 5, it projects the outer character of love and harmony (6) through the inner influences of new beginnings (1) of change (5). At its higher vibration, the 15/6 is the ambassador of love committed to benevolent causes and a champion for the greater good. At its lower level, the 15/6 tends to meddle in affairs of the heart, taking it upon themselves to "fix" other people's problems and relationships.

51/6—Makeover Expert

When the 6 appears from the sum of 5 and 1, it projects the outer character of love and harmony (6) through the inner influences of change (5) of new beginnings (1). At its higher vibration, the 51/6 is the makeover expert with a gift for reinventing identity, enhancing image, and bringing out the best in people and situations. At its lower level, the 51/6 can be very self-sacrificing to the point of losing their identity for the sake of others.

24/6—Marriage Counselor

When the 6 appears from the sum of 2 and 4, it projects the outer character of love and harmony (6) through the inner influences of duality (2) of structure and stability (4). At its higher vibration, the 24/6 is the marriage counselor, able to facilitate the mutual understanding and compromise upon which successful relationships are built. At its lower level, the 24/6 is cautious in love and emotionally guarded. This makes them hesitant to being vulnerable and getting close.

42/6—Match Maker

When the 6 appears from the sum of 4 and 2, it projects the outer character of love and harmony (6) through the inner influences of structure and stability (4) of duality (2). At its higher vibration, the 42/6 is the matchmaker with a knack for creating partnerships that work and providing support to make them last. At its lower level, the 42/6 can be cynical and disillusioned in affairs of the heart, assuming relationships are inherently unstable and prone to conflict.

33—Master Catalyst

See page 138 for the meaning of this master number.

60/6—Hopeful Romantic

When the 6 appears from the sum of 6 and 0, it projects the outer character of love and harmony (6) through the inner influences of harmony (6) of potential (0). At its highest vibration, the 60/6 is the hopeful romantic who sees the potential for love in all situations and for good in all people. Able to bring compassion to the most desperate of circumstances, the 60/6 is a true emissary of hope. At its lower expression, the 60/6 is the *hopeless* romantic that is desperate for love and becomes infatuated easily. It tends to see everything and everyone with rose-colored glasses, their idealistic innocence easily taken advantage of.

7 · Truth

Positive Qualities: Knowledgeable, authentic, purposeful, devout, spiritual

Negative Tendencies: Pretentious, over-analytical, skeptical, preachy, fanatical, elitist

Overall Personality of the 7 Vibration

The first half of the base-12 cycle of learning enabled us to discover love. From this point on in our journey, each energy becomes a higher frequency reflection of the earlier energies through the compassionate mirror of the 6 of love. This enables us to see in a more selfless humanitarian light and expand love beyond ourselves.

The first energy we encounter beyond the 6 is the 7 of spiritual truth and knowledge. By far the most profound change we can experience, the 7 of spiritual awakening is the enlightened reflection of the 5 of physical change and the polarity of the 1 of our physical awakening at birth.

Still, as with all energies, it's up to us how far we wish to open the door at 7, if at all. The yearning for knowledge and truth still drives the 7 whether or not spirituality inclined. Although spiritual belief is by no means a requirement for a meaningful life, denying our divinity can leave us feeling less than we are and limit our potential for growth. If we choose to walk through that door, however, we can reconnect with our higher self and gain a peace and contentment that transcends ego. Our awakened perspective inspires us to then apply that spiritual knowing through the 8 of manifestation for the greater good.

What It Means When a 7 Appears as . . .

7—Seeker of Truth

When the 7 appears on its own, not from the reduction of a two-digit number, it projects the outer character of the 7 directly rather than in a roundabout way. This is the energy of truth and knowledge. At its higher vibration, the 7 is the seeker of spiritual truth who embraces their divinity and is dedicated to spiritual growth and the raising of consciousness. At its lower expression, the 7 is the intellectual seeker of knowledge that tends to be skeptical of anything it can't see or touch. It can come across as pretentious, self-righteous, and a know-it-all. This makes it difficult for them to get out of their head long enough to feel their emotions, their connection to their higher self.

16/7—Compassionate Messenger of Truth

When the 7 appears from the sum of 1 and 6, it projects the outer character of truth and knowledge (7) through the inner influences of new beginnings (1) of love and harmony (6). At its higher vibration, the 16/7 is the compassionate messenger of spiritual truth and knowledge. At its lower level, the 16/7 can become overzealous in spreading their well-intended message of love to those not ready to hear.

61/7—Harmonizer of Truth

When the 7 appears from the sum of 6 and 1, it projects the outer character of truth and knowledge (7) through the inner influences of love and harmony (6) of new beginnings (1). At its higher vibration, the 61/7 is the spiritual harmonizer that utilizes their knowledge to bring harmony and love to new and unfamiliar situations. At its lower level, the 61/7 can become a self-appointed missionary that imposes their beliefs on others and causes more disruption.

25/7—Mentor of Truth

When the 7 appears from the sum of 2 and 5, it projects the outer character of truth and knowledge (7) through the inner influences of the duality (2) of change (5). At its higher vibration, the 25/7 is the mentor of spiritual truth that understands the physical-spiritual duality of spiritual growth and uses that knowledge to coach others. At its lower level, the 25/7 is spiritually cautious, fearful of what such change may involve.

52/7—Negotiator of Truth

When the 7 appears from the sum of 5 and 2, it projects the outer character of truth and knowledge (7) through the inner influences of the change (5) of duality (2). At its higher vibration, the 52/7 is the spiritual negotiator able to bring balance to conflicted situations in an enlightened way. At its lower level, the 52/7 is the religious evangelist looking to convert others to their doctrine, only to create separation and conflict between belief systems.

34/7—Teacher of Truth

When the 7 appears from the sum of 3 and 4, it projects the outer character of truth and knowledge (7) through the inner influences of the catalyst (3) of structure and stability (4). At its higher vibration, the 34/7 is the spiritual teacher who provides a structured and safe learning environment for exploring spirituality. At its lower level, the 34/7 is the strict schoolmaster that imposes too much structure and rigidity to the learning process.

43/7—Guardian of Truth

When the 7 appears from the sum of 4 and 3, it projects the outer character of truth and knowledge (7) through the inner influences of the structure and stability (4) of the catalyst (3). At its higher vibration, the 43/7 is the guardian of spiritual truth that provides structure and methodology to spiritual teaching. At its lower level, the 43/7 is the bureaucratic administrator who micromanages the teaching process.

70/7—Visionary of Truth

When the 7 appears from the sum of 7 and 0, it projects the outer character of truth and knowledge (7) through the inner influences of truth and knowledge (7) of potential (0). At its highest vibration, the 70/7 is the spiritual visionary who sees every situation as an opportunity for learning and growth and knows how to maximize that opportunity. At its lowest, the 70/7 is the directionless student that searches for knowledge but doesn't focus long enough to learn.

8 · Manifestation

Positive Qualities: Abundant, productive, practical, physically/ spiritually balanced, grateful

Negative Tendencies: Lacking, materialistic, ambitious, entitled, extravagant, wasteful

Overall Personality of the 8 Vibration

Where the 4 represents structure, stability, and security in our own lives, the 8 is its enlightened reflection that seeks structure and stability for the welfare of others. The 8 is the resourceful builder that manifests physical-spiritual balance in practical ways. It is also the opposite polarity of the 2 of physical duality and balance.

Those who embody the higher qualities of the 8 work to create a lasting legacy of benefit to society rather than acquiring wealth for the few. The 8 is the vibrational signature of the benevolent benefactor who knows the difference between governance and greed, responsibility and results, the "human" and "resources." The effective 8 recognizes the talent and potential in others and is an advocate for sustainability and conservation in all things. Not afraid of challenge or hard work, the 8 is a resilient energy that exemplifies perseverance, dedication, and excellence. Through the service and practical contributions of the 8, the 9 of completion becomes a celebration of a job well done or a life well lived.

What It Means When an 8 Appears as ...

8—Builder

When the 8 appears on its own, not from the reduction of a two-digit number, it projects the outer character of the 8 directly rather than in a roundabout way. This is the energy of abundance and manifestation. At its higher vibration, the 8 is the benevolent builder. Capable and considerate, the enlightened 8 works hard to build a better place for everyone and utilizes resources in an efficient and sensitive way. At its lower vibration, the 8 can be materialistic, entitled, and power hungry. Driven for "more" rather than "enough," the greedy 8 places their own interests above others, including the welfare of the natural environment.

17/8—Builder of Truth

When the 8 appears from the sum of 1 and 7, it projects the outer character of abundance and manifestation (8) through the inner influences of new beginnings (1) of truth and knowledge (7). At its higher vibration, the 17/8 is the builder of spiritual truth and knowledge that is skilled in helping others tap into their gifts. At its lower level, the 17/8 hoards knowledge and acquires abundance for themselves.

71/8—Builder of Foundations

When the 8 appears from the sum of 7 and 1, it projects the outer character of abundance and manifestation (8) through the inner influences of truth and knowledge (7) of new beginnings (1). At its higher vibration, the 71/8 is the builder of foundations that creates a secure and solid footing for those just learning how to manifest. Able to see things for what they are, the practical 71/8 provides the support and guidance to translate ideas into concrete form. At its lower level, the 71/8 is always searching for the angle to get ahead, jumping from one get-rich-quick scheme to another and taking advantage of the inexperience of others along the way.

26/8—Builder of Relationships

When the 8 appears from the sum of 2 and 6, it projects the outer character of abundance and manifestation (8) through the inner influences of the duality (2) of love and harmony (6). At its higher vibration, the 26/8 is the benevolent builder of relationships able to create solid and lasting partnerships and mutually beneficial outcomes. Skilled at finding balance and facilitating compromise, the capable 26/8 remains reasonable and resilient in the most challenging of situations. At its lower level, the 26/8 creates conflict and division, putting obstacles in the way of others in order to gain an advantage.

62/8—Renovator

When the 8 appears from the sum of 6 and 2, it projects the outer character of abundance and manifestation (8) through the inner influences of love and harmony (6) of duality (2). At its higher vibration, the 62/8 is the resourceful renovator, able to restore harmony to dysfunctional situations that others consider unsalvageable. At its lower level, the 62/8 is the shady contractor who appears above board but cuts corners behind the scenes.

35/8—Developer

When the 8 appears from the sum of 3 and 5, it projects the outer character of abundance and manifestation (8) through the inner influences of the catalyst (3) of change (5). At its higher vibration, the 35/8 is the progressive developer with a keen eye for value and a knack for transforming the ordinary into something exceptional. At its lower level, the 35/8 is the persistent salesman that pressures others into buying what he's selling.

53/8—Market Analyst

When the 8 appears from the sum of 5 and 3, it projects the outer character of abundance and manifestation (8) through the inner influences of change (5) of the catalyst (3). At its higher vibration, the 53/8 is the market analyst able to anticipate changing conditions and trends and capitalize on that change. At its lower level, the 53/8 is the market manipulator who tries to influence situations and spread disinformation for his own benefit.

44—Mastery of Structure

See page 139 for the meaning of this master number.

80/8—Life Coach

When the 8 appears from the sum of 8 and 0, it projects the outer character of abundance and manifestation (8) through the inner influences of abundance and manifestation (8) of potential (0). At its highest vibration, the 80/8 is the motivational life coach with a gift for empowering others to achieve their dreams. At its lowest, the 80/8 is the slick motivational speaker that tells people what they want to hear and endears himself into their wallets.

9 · Completion

Positive Qualities: Fulfilled, content, accepting, forgiving, humanitarian, selfless, dedicated

Negative Tendencies: Unfulfilled, defeated, vengeful, regretful, fatalistic, relentless

Overall Personality of the 9 Vibration

The 9 is the energy of completion and endings, of finishing what we start, and achieving our goals and moving on. A mature energy of taking responsibility for one's actions, the 9 is the enlightened reflection and opposite polarity of the catalytic 3 of blaming outside influences.

The higher 9 finds joy and closure in completion: a wonderful vacation enjoyed to the fullest, the timely conclusion of a meaningful relationship, or the celebration of a life well lived of someone dear. The lower 9 vibration, conversely, is often experienced with sadness and loss: the vacation that ended too soon, the painful end of a relationship, or the traumatic loss of a loved one. Thus, without the compassionate perspective of the 6 of love, the 9 becomes the 9 – 6 = 3 of impersonal catalytic disruption.

Regardless, the 9 always brings us to the end of one path and the start of another. For those on a spiritual quest to know more, the 9 helps us move beyond our illusion of separation and self and toward humanitarian selflessness. It is this selfless outlook that enables us to see clearly at the 10 of awareness.

What It Means When a 9 Appears as...

9—Humanitarian

When the 9 appears on its own and not from the reduction of a two-digit number, it projects the outer character of the 9 directly rather than in a roundabout way. This is the energy of completion. At its higher vibration, the 9 is the humanitarian who appreciates the value of everything they have experienced as opportunities for growth and learning, exemplifying that mature acceptance and objective wisdom for others. At its lower vibration, the 9 can feel defeated and pessimistic at one extreme or impatient and stubborn at the other, quick to end things that aren't going their way or refusing to let go when it's time to move on.

18/9—Generous Humanitarian

When the 9 appears from the sum of 1 and 8, it projects the outer character of completion (9) through the inner influences of new beginnings (1) of manifestation and abundance (8). At its higher vibration, the 18/9 is the generous humanitarian who is dedicated to helping others succeed by showing how to manifest abundance in their own lives. This includes selflessly sharing their talent for physical manifestation as well as their spiritually abundant outlook. At its lower level, the 18/9 is the wealthy miser that hoards abundance for themselves as their only end.

81/9—Innovative Humanitarian

When the 9 appears from the sum of 8 and 1, it projects the outer character of completion (9) through the inner influences of manifestation (8) of new beginnings (1). At its higher vibration, the 81/9 is the innovative humanitarian who feels complete by manifesting new beginnings and opportunities for the benefit of others. At its lower level, the 81/9 is the obsessive inventor who only feels content when manifesting something new and innovative.

27/9—Balanced Humanitarian

When the 9 appears from the sum of 2 and 7, it projects the outer character of completion (9) through the inner influences of the duality (2) of truth and knowledge (7). At its higher vibration, the 27/9 is the balanced humanitarian who understands the physical-spiritual duality and balance inherent in a spiritually complete life and shares that knowledge with others. At its lower level, the 27/9 uses knowledge in a competitive and conditional way to accomplish what they want.

72/9—Resilient Humanitarian

When the 9 appears from the sum of 7 and 2, it projects the outer character of completion (9) through the inner influences of truth and knowledge (7) of duality (2). At its higher vibration, the 72/9 is the resilient humanitarian who understands the value of contrast and polarity for revealing truth and exemplifies that strength of character for others. At its lower level, the 72/9 is quick to feel defeated and give up, dwelling on the negative and what could go wrong. This negativity can also be expressed in a malicious way by causing conflict to prevent others from achieving their goals.

36/9—Compassionate Humanitarian

When the 9 appears from the sum of 3 and 6, it projects the outer character of completion (9) through the inner influences of the catalyst (3) of love (6). At its higher vibration, the 36/9 is the compassionate humanitarian that provides completion and closure in situations involving endings. At its lower level, the 36/9 can be manipulative in affairs of the heart and steer relationships to serve their own ends.

63/9—Creative Humanitarian

When the 9 appears from the sum of 6 and 3, it projects the outer character of completion (9) through the inner influences of harmony and love (6) of the catalyst (3). At its higher vibration, the 63/9 is the creative humanitarian with a gift for communication able to bring closure and acceptance in creative and impactful ways. At its lower level, the 63/9 is an influence peddler and meddler who loves to mix things up to get their own way.

45/9—Humanitarian Organizer

When the 9 appears from the sum of 4 and 5, it projects the outer character of completion (9) through the inner influences of structure and stability (4) of change (5). At its higher vibration, the 45/9 is the humanitarian organizer able to facilitate change in an orderly way and coordinate the efficient completion of activities. At its lower level, the 45/9 attempts to get their own way by choreo-graphing how situations play out and micromanaging others.

54/9—Humanitarian Rebuilder

When the 9 appears from the sum of 5 and 4, it projects the outer charac-ter of completion (9) through the inner influences of change (5) of structure and stability (4). At its higher vibration, the 54/9 is the humanitarian rebuilder skilled at restructuring dysfunctional systems and situations to serve the greater good. At its lower level, the 54/9 is a systems buster who causes disruption to put an end to things it doesn't like.

90/9—Humanitarian Visionary

When the 9 appears from the sum of 9 and 0, it projects the outer charac-ter of completion (9) through the inner influences of completion (9) of poten-tial (0). At its higher expression, the 90/9 is the humanitarian visionary able to bring out the full potential in situations and people. At its lower level, the 90/9 seeks to interfere with others by restricting their potential and undermining their accomplishments.

10 · Awareness

Positive Qualities: Insightful, intuitive, perceptive, open minded, curious, focused

Negative Tendencies: Distracted, confused, prying, paranoid, selective, obsessive

Overall Personality of the 10 Vibration

The perspective and wisdom gained from our many experiences from 1 to 9 are integrated at the 10 of awareness and insight. A secure and self-aware frequency, the 10 represents our ability to see clearly and to acknowledge the thoughts and beliefs we hold each moment to determine the potential we manifest as our reality.

The 10 signifies a new relationship with ourselves, of stepping into our power as conscious cocreators of everything we experience and holding ourselves to that higher standard. As the enlightened reflection of the 2 of duality, the 10 objectively sees through the contrast and polarity in situations to the vibrational insight that duality provides. As such, where the 2 represents outer peace, 10 is of inner peace of mind. And, as the polarized opposite of the 4 of physical structure and security, the 10 reaches beyond to explore the structure of higher consciousness. It is through the clarity of the 10 that we can fully understand the lessons illuminated by the 11.

What It Means When a 10 Appears as ...

10—Intuitive

When the 10 appears on its own and not from the reduction of a two-digit number, it projects the outer character of the 10 directly rather than in a roundabout way. This is the energy of awareness and insight. At its higher vibration, the 10 is the gifted intuitive whose connection to their higher consciousness is strong and who sees the truth and potential for learning in all experiences. At its lower vibration, the 10 can become unfocused and overwhelmed by its ability to perceive so much.

19/10—Intuitive Facilitator

When the 10 appears from the sum of 1 and 9, it projects the outer character of awareness and insight (10) through the inner influences of new beginnings (1) of completion (9). At its higher vibration, the 19/10 is the intuitive facilitator able to assess situations and people quickly and accurately and use that insight to bring things to their appropriate conclusion. This is the person others go to when they want to get to the bottom of things quickly. At its lower level, the 19/10 sees everything as temporary and finite with a beginning (1) and end (9) and can become quite fatalistic and uninspired as a result.

91/10—Intuitive Innovator

When the 10 appears from the sum of 9 and 1, it projects the outer character of awareness and insight (10) through the inner influences of completion (9) of new beginnings (1). At its higher vibration, the 91/10 is the intuitive innovator that gets frequent inspiration for promising ideas and a talent for getting those ideas off the ground. At its lower level, the 91/10 is a great starter but poor finisher, heading off in many directions but following through on very little so distracted are they.

28/10—Intuitive Manifester

When the 10 appears from the sum of 2 and 8, it projects the outer character of awareness and insight (10) through the inner influences of the duality (2) of manifestation and abundance (8). At its higher vibration, the 28/10 is the intuitive manifester that understands that true abundance comes from physical-spiritual balance and helps others achieve that balanced perspective in their own lives. At its lower level, the 28/10 believes that resources are limited and that manifesting abundance must be competitive with winners and losers. This materialistic view of abundance attracts a revolving door of personal gain and loss until this lesson is integrated.

82/<u>10</u>—Intuitive Matchmaker

When the <u>10</u> appears from the sum of 8 and 2, it projects the outer character of awareness and insight (<u>10</u>) through the inner influences of manifestation (8) of duality (2). At its higher vibration, the 82/<u>10</u> is the intuitive matchmaker who creates balance and successful relationships through their keen eye for compatibility and synergy. At its lower level, the 82/<u>10</u> creates conflict and opposition for their own benefit in a very intentional way.

37/<u>10</u>—Intuitive Teacher

When the <u>10</u> appears from the sum of 3 and 7, it projects the outer character of awareness and insight (<u>10</u>) through the inner influences of the catalyst (3) of truth and knowledge (7). At its higher vibration, the 37/<u>10</u> is the intuitive teacher who creates awareness by encouraging spiritual exploration and higher learning. At its lower level, the 37/<u>10</u> is the snobbish intellectual who brags about their extensive knowledge to stroke their own ego and to make others feel inferior.

73/<u>10</u>—Intuitive Strategist

When the <u>10</u> appears from the sum of 7 and 3, it projects the outer character of awareness and insight (<u>10</u>) through the inner influences of truth and knowledge (7) of the catalyst (3). At its higher vibration, the 73/<u>10</u> is the intuitive strategist who has keen insight into what makes things tick and how to guide things for the greatest good. At its lower expression, the 73/<u>10</u> uses their perceptiveness in a manipulative and self-serving way.

46/<u>10</u>—Compassionate Intuitive

When the <u>10</u> appears from the sum of 4 and 6, it projects the outer character of awareness and insight (<u>10</u>) through the inner influences of the structure and stability (4) of harmony and love (6). At its higher vibration, the 46/<u>10</u> is the compassionate intuitive who creates organizations and initiatives that bring awareness to the welfare of others. At its lower level, the 46/<u>10</u> is the mother hen who tries to take everyone under her wing thinking she knows best. Although this is usually done in kindness, the lower 46/<u>10</u> can be quite meddling and suffocating.

64/<u>10</u>—Intuitive Architect

When the <u>10</u> appears from the sum of 6 and 4, it projects the outer character of awareness and insight (<u>10</u>) through the inner influences of harmony and love (6) of structure and stability (4). At its higher vibration, the 64/<u>10</u> is the intuitive architect with a gift for building harmony and love into lasting form. At its lower level, the 64/<u>10</u> is obsessed with structure and order itself and expects others to follow that rigid worldview and protocol.

55—Mastery of Change

See page 140 for the meaning of this master number.

<u>100</u>/<u>10</u>—Oracle

When the <u>10</u> appears from the sum of <u>10</u> and 0, it projects the outer character of awareness and insight (<u>10</u>) through the inner influences of awareness (<u>10</u>) of potential (0). At its higher expression, the <u>100</u>/<u>10</u> is the intuitive oracle who has a deep awareness of potentials and can provide profound insight for tapping into that potential. At its lower level, the <u>100</u>/<u>10</u> can lose touch with reality and become quite disconnected from the practical aspects of life.

11 · Illumination

Positive Qualities: Understanding, knowing, receptive, wise, inspired

Negative Tendencies: Oblivious, unreceptive, naïve, disillusioned, ignorant

Overall Personality of the 11 Vibration

From the aware and perceptive energy of the 10, we achieve illumination at the 11—the vibration of profound realization, "aha!" moments and finally getting it.

Although illumination often occurs suddenly and dramatically, the learning and preparation leading up to it does not. Illumination is the energetic culmination of all our experiences such that we can see ourselves in what happens around us. The 11 is the enlightened reflection of the 1 looking outward and recognizing itself, of reality reflecting our beliefs, of the physical seeing the spiritual without distortion. The elevated 11 of change in perspective is also the opposite polarity of the reactive 5 of change in circumstances.

Still, the 11 possesses the same inherent duality as any of the numbers of our vibrational journey. Those who recognize themselves in others understand the real lesson being illuminated, while those still in the shadow of fear see only more fear and further separation of the solitary 1. As such, the 11 has great power to unify or divide.

What It Means When an 11 Appears as . . .

11—Luminary

When the 11 appears on its own and not from the reduction of a two-digit number, it projects the outer character of the 11 directly rather than in a roundabout way. This is the energy of illumination. At its higher vibration, the 11 is the luminary that understands the deeper meaning within experiences and inspires others through their wise and awakened example.

At its lower vibration, the <u>11</u> can feel polarized by events that illuminate what they are afraid to see in themselves. When we avoid acknowledging the darker aspects of ourselves highlighted by events that mirror those weaknesses, we create further separation and fear that perpetuates the pattern. We will keep attracting those same polarized lessons until we look inward and change our limiting beliefs.

1<u>10</u>/<u>11</u>—Luminary of Awareness

When the <u>11</u> appears from the sum of 1 and <u>10</u>, it projects the outer character of illumination (<u>11</u>) through the inner influences of new beginnings (1) of awareness (<u>10</u>). At its higher vibration, the 1<u>10</u>/<u>11</u> is the luminary of awareness that shows leadership in expanding awareness and shining light on the truth. At its lower level, the 1<u>10</u>/<u>11</u> is the shrewd operative who uses their keen insight to gain valuable intelligence for their own benefit and to spread misinformation to mislead others.

<u>10</u>1/<u>11</u>—Luminary of Innovation

When the <u>11</u> appears from the sum of <u>10</u> and 1, it projects the outer character of illumination (<u>11</u>) through the inner influences of awareness (<u>10</u>) of new beginnings (1). At its higher vibration, the <u>10</u>1/<u>11</u> is the luminary of innovation whose inspirational leadership and intuitive understanding of transforming ideas into reality serves as a trailblazer for inspiring others. At its lower level, the <u>10</u>1/<u>11</u> is the know-it-all who seeks to impress others with their broad knowledge of many subjects rather than putting that intelligence to good use.

29/<u>11</u>—Luminary of Completion

When the <u>11</u> appears from the sum of 2 and 9, it projects the outer character of illumination (<u>11</u>) through the inner influences of duality (2) of completion (9). At its higher vibration, the 29/<u>11</u> is the luminary of completion who understands that every ending brings with it the potential for both grief and closure and how to gently counsel others through such transitional situations.

At its lower level, the 29/11 is aggressively competitive and must win at all cost. It thrives in the limelight and tends to have a superiority complex.

92/11—Luminary of Peace

When the 11 appears from the sum of 9 and 2, it projects the outer character of illumination (11) through the inner influences of completion (9) of duality (2). At its higher vibration, the 92/11 is the luminary of peace who uses their wisdom to end conflict, negotiate peace and bring calm. At its lower level, the 92/11 strays to the opposite extreme, using their shrewd wits to eliminate any competition through brute force.

38/11—Luminary of Abundance

When the 11 appears from the sum of 3 and 8, it projects the outer character of illumination (11) through the inner influences of the catalyst (3) of abundance (8). At its higher vibration, the 38/11 is the luminary of abundance who uses their wisdom in a benevolent way to create growth and abundance for the greater good. At its lower level, the 38/11 is the empire builder who seeks unlimited personal wealth and power.

83/11—Luminary of Creativity

When the 11 appears from the sum of 8 and 3, it projects the outer character of illumination (11) through the inner influences of the manifestation (8) of catalysts (3). At its higher vibration, the 83/11 is the luminary of creativity who knows how to manifest creativity in clever ways and serve as a shining light for others. At its lower level, the 83/11 manifests turmoil and discord, stirring the pot for their own benefit or just because they can.

47/11—Luminary of Knowledge

When the 11 appears from the sum of 4 and 7, it projects the outer character of illumination (11) through the inner influences of the structure (4) of truth and knowledge (7). At its higher expression, the 47/11 is the luminary of knowledge who uses their wisdom to create stability and structure for learning, both academically and spiritually. At its lower level, the 47/11 is a rigid school-master who attempts to control how and what others learn.

74/11—Luminary of Structure

When the 11 appears from the sum of 7 and 4, it projects the outer character of illumination (11) through the inner influences of the truth and knowledge (7) of structure (4). At its higher expression, the 74/11 is the luminary of structure who has a deep understanding of structure, organization, and systems and a talent for imparting that knowledge to others. At its lower level, the 74/11 uses their knowledge of structure and order in a narrow-minded way, imposing their view that their way is the only way.

56/11—Luminary of Love

When the 11 appears from the sum of 5 and 6, it projects the outer character of illumination (11) through the inner influences of the change and exploration (5) of harmony and love (6). At its higher expression, the 56/11 is the luminary of love able to create harmony and explore love in an inspirational way. At its lower level, the 56/11 is fickle and restless in matters of love, seeing only the risk of a broken heart and being hurt. They avoid commitment and don't allow themselves to be vulnerable as a result.

65/11—Luminary of Change

When the 11 appears from the sum of 6 and 5, it projects the outer character of illumination (11) through the inner influences of harmony and love (6) of change (5). At its higher level, the 65/11 is the luminary of change who inspires others through their unshakable courage and adventurous spirit. At its lower level, the 65/11 is an adrenaline junky and risk-taker who never sits still, always looking for their next thrill ride regardless how perilous.

110/11—Luminary of Potential

When the <u>11</u> appears from the sum of <u>11</u> and 0, it projects the outer character of illumination (<u>11</u>) through the inner influences of the illumination (<u>11</u>) of potential (0). At its higher expression, the <u>110/11</u> is the luminary of potential who sees hidden value and possibilities that others miss and inspires others to express their own untapped potential. At its lower level, the <u>110/11</u> is easily overwhelmed by the seemingly endless possibilities, choices, and challenges that life presents.

11 · Mastery of Self

Unreduced Qualities: Self-aware, idealistic visionary, authentic, honest, inspirational

Reduced Qualities (of the 1 + 1 = 2): Peaceful, cooperative, balanced, fair, social

Negative Tendencies (of the 2): Competitive, critical, adversarial, judgmental, defensive

What It Means When Master Number 11 Appears

Master 11s have mastered the balance between ego and their higher self and exemplify authenticity, transparency, and truth. They know who they are and act with integrity and grace, serving others selflessly and joyfully.

Master 11s are idealists and visionaries who also tend to be impractical and unrealistic, downshifting to the peaceful 1 + 1 = 2 of duality and balance when not fully engaged. When unable to express their gifts, the easily frustrated 11 can descend quickly to the negative extremes of the 2, either outwardly in the form of competitiveness, defensiveness, and conflict or inwardly as self-doubt and insecurity.

Examples of Master 11

Expression number (birth name) of Albert Einstein, the physicist who developed the theory of relativity and discovered the equivalence of energy and matter: $132524\ 51534515 = 15/\ 6 + 25/7 = 6 + 7 = $ master 11.

Electricity, the flow of singular electrons as the smallest unit of charge: $5 + 3 + 5 + 3 + 2 + 9 + 9 + 3 + 9 + 2 + 7 = 4\mathrm{x}12 + 9 = 4 + 9 = 1\mathrm{x}12 + 1 = $ master 11.

Soul, our enlightened higher self $= 1 + 6 + 3 + 3 = 1\mathrm{x}12 + 1 = $ master 11.

22 · Mastery of Duality

Unreduced Qualities: Master builder, practical visionary, physical-spiritual balance, generous

Reduced Qualities (of the 2+2 = 4): Stable, secure, dependable, practical, responsible

Negative Tendencies (of the 4): Inflexible, stubborn, cautious, perfectionist, private, unrealistic

What It Means When Master Number 22 Appears

Master 22s are master builders who exemplify physical-spiritual balance and can translate this in practical ways for the greater good. The 22 possesses all the attributes of the 11 but is also able to manifest the personal idealism and vision of the 11 into concrete form.

So capable is the 22 that it needs to avoid becoming an empire builder for the sake of power and feeling superior to others. The 22 downshifts to the stable and dependable 2 + 2 = 4 when not actively engaged but can go the extremes of the 4 when unable to pursue their ambitious dreams. This can make them quite reclusive, inflexible, and risk averse, retreating to the safety and security of their private world.

Examples of Master 22

Life path (birth date) for Marie Curie, the pioneering physicist and chemist who explored radioactivity, discovered two elements, and won two Nobel Prizes: Birth date = 11 7 1867 in base-10 = 11 + 7 + 10117/17/8 in base-12 = 11 + 7 + 8 = master 22.

Carbon, the fundamental element upon which all organic life is built, capable of extreme properties from the softness of graphite to the hardness of diamond: 3 + 1 + 9 + 2 + 6 + 5 = 2x12 + 2 = master 22.

Cosmic, that which relates to the universe and everything within it: 3 + 6 + 1 + 4 + 9 + 3 = 2x12 + 2 = master 22.

33 · Master Catalyst

Unreduced Qualities: Master healer and teacher, motivational, compassionate

Reduced Qualities (of the 3 + 3 = 6): Loving, caring, kind, supportive, accepting

Negative Tendencies (of the 6): Self-sacrificing, submissive, meddling, needy, oversensitive

What It Means When Master Number 33 Appears

Master 33s are the master teachers and healers who inspire compassion and love through their enlightened example and magnetic presence. The highly catalytic vibration of the 33 possesses all the idealistic vision of the 11 and the practical generosity of the 22 but also the ability to share it with others in an empowering and loving way. In this way, the 33 enables others to realize their own gifts of expression and to be catalysts of growth themselves.

When their exemplary gifts are not fully expressed, the 33 downshifts to the loving and harmonious nature of the 3 + 3 = 6. As with all master numbers, this lower octave of the 6 can stray to the extreme. This can result in profound self-sacrifice, submission, neediness, and keeping harmony at all cost. However, the 33 is such an enlightened and mature vibration that it reverberates as the powerful catalyst of compassion even in its darkest hours.

Examples of Master 33

Apollo 13, one of the most influential missions of the early space program: $(1 + 7 + 6 + 3 + 3 + 6) + (13) = (2 \times 12 + 2) + (1 \times 12 + 1) = $ master 22 + master 11 = master 33.

Gravity, a fundamental force of nature and master catalyst that enables matter to form and life to exist: $7 + 9 + 1 + 4 + 9 + 2 + 7 = 3 \times 12 + 3 = $ master 33.

44 · Mastery of Structure

Unreduced Qualities: Master engineer, creator of structure, stability, natural order

Reduced Qualities (of the 4+4 = 8): Capable, productive, efficient, abundant, generous

Negative Tendencies (of the 8): Lacking, entitled, materialistic, ambitious, extravagant

What It Means When Master Number 44 Appears

Master 44s are the experts of structure and of creating stability and order for the betterment of society and the planet. They intuitively know how things work and their underlying design and processes. This enables the master 44 to simplify the complex down to its fundamental essence and to apply that understanding to achieving sustainable balance. As with each master number, the 44 possesses all the qualities of the lower master numbers from 11 to 33 plus a higher octave of potential.

When their full mastery is not being expressed, the 44 downshifts to the practical and generous 4 + 4 = 8 of manifestation and abundance. However, when misguided, the 44 has the potential to stray to the lower tendencies of the 8 vibration of being materialistic, extravagant, impatient, demanding, and entitled.

Examples of Master 44

Current name number for Leonardo da Vinci, the multitalented Italian Renaissance artist, scientist, and inventor: $(3 + 5 + 6 + 5 + 1 + 9 + 4 + 6) + (4 + 1) + (4 + 9 + 5 + 3 + 9) = (3x12 + 3) + 5 + (2x12 + 6)$ = master $33 + 5 + 26/8$ = master 44.

Scientific, methodical/systematic: $1 + 3 + 9 + 5 + 5 + 2 + 9 + 6 + 9 + 3 = 4x12 + 4$ = master 44.

Technology, the application of scientific knowledge for practical purposes: $2 + 5 + 3 + 8 + 5 + 6 + 3 + 6 + 7 + 7 = 4x12 + 4$ = master 44.

55 · Mastery of Change

Unreduced Qualities: Master of change and growth, absolute allowance and trust, fearless

Reduced Qualities (of the 5 + 5 = <u>10</u>): Insightful, intuitive, perceptive, open minded, objective

Negative Tendencies (of the <u>10</u>): Distracted, prying, confused, paranoid, selective, obsessive

What It Means When Master Number 55 Appears

Master 55s are the fearless trailblazers who embrace change and welcome the unknown. They are the first to venture somewhere new and to find safe passage for others to follow. Placing the welfare of others ahead of their own, they are the embodiment of selfless service. As with each master number, the 55 possesses all the qualities of the lower master numbers from 11 to 44 plus a higher octave of potential.

When their enlightened mastery is not being expressed, the 55 downshifts to the intuitive and perceptive 5 + 5 = <u>10</u> of awareness and insight. However, when restricted or frustrated, the 55 can stray to the lower tendencies of the <u>10</u> vibration of being prying and selective but in a very intense, obsessive, and invasive way. Napoleon Bonaparte's expression number (birth name) has this extreme vibration, though not as a master 55: $(5 + 1 + 7 + 6 + 3 + 5 + 6 + 5) + (2 + 6 + 5 + 1 + 7 + 1 + 9 + 2 + 5) = (3x12 + 2) + (3x12 + 2) = 32/5 + 32/5 = 5 + 5 = \underline{10}$.

Examples of Master 55

Quantum mechanics, theory of physics that describes the behavior of energy and matter at the smallest scales: $(8 + 3 + 1 + 5 + 2 + 3 + 4) + (4 + 5 + 3 + 8 + 1 + 5 + 9 + 3 + 1) = (2x12 + 2) + (3x12 + 3) =$ master 22 + master 33 = master 55.

Periodic table, listing of all elements by atomic structure and properties: $(7 + 5 + 9 + 9 + 6 + 4 + 9 + 3) + (2 + 1 + 2 + 3 + 5) = (4 \times 12 + 4) + (1 \times 12 + 1) =$ master 44 + master 11 = master 55.

66 · Mastery of Love

Unreduced Qualities: Unconditional love

Reduced Qualities (of the 6 + 6 = 10/1): Hopeful, optimistic, enthusiastic, inspiring

Negative Tendencies (of the 10/1): Selfish, arrogant, aggressive, self-critical, fearful, isolated, vulnerable

What It Means When Master Number 66 Appears

The master 66 is the frequency of unconditional love, the purest form of love of all. It is that sense of absolute joy, fulfillment, and inner harmony we feel when we hold unconditional love for ourselves or others: a parent's love for their child, an organ donor's gift to a stranger in need, a firefighter risking their own life to save another. It is such an elevated energy that it is difficult to sustain for long while in the lower density of our physical form.

As explained on page 88, master number 66 is where polarity no longer exists, as it is the singularity of love at the very heart of the base-12 numerology cycle. It is the only still point within the human experience in which everything seems possible, a state only otherwise achieved at the 0 of potential upon our return to spirit.

When the master 66 is in lower throttle, which is most of the time, it downshifts to 6 + 6 = 1x12 + 0 = 10/1 of new beginnings (1) through new beginnings (1) of potential (0), a beacon of hope and optimism whose very presence uplifts others. When unable to express itself, the 66 can exhibit the negative tendencies of the 10/1 listed above.

Example of Master 66

Expression number of Michelangelo di Lodovico Buonarroti Simoni, Italian Renaissance sculptor, painter, architect, and poet: $(4 + 9 + 3 + 8 + 5 + 3 + 1 + 5 + 7 + 5 + 3 + 6) + (4 + 9) + (3 + 6 + 4 + 6 + 4 + 9 + 3 + 6) + (2 + 3 + 6 + 5 + 1 + 9 + 9 + 6 + 2 + 9) + (1 + 9 + 4 + 6 + 5 + 9) = (4x12 + \underline{11}) + (1x12 + 1) + (3x12 + 5) + (4x12 + 4) + (2x12 + \underline{10}) = 4\underline{11}/13/4 +$ master 11 $+ 35/8 +$ master 44 $+ 10/1 =$ master 66.

77 · Mastery of Truth

Unreduced Qualities: Absolute knowledge

Reduced Qualities (of the 7 + 7 = 12/3): Influential, motivational, creative, communicative

Negative Tendencies (of the 12/3): Manipulative, opinionated, pushy, meddling, deceptive

What It Means When Master Number 77 Appears

The master 77 is the frequency of absolute knowledge and spiritual truth, of profound knowing. We touch this highly elevated energy more often that we think, particularly when we allow our intuition to be heard. That sudden flash of knowing who is going to call before the phone rings, the gut feeling you get about a person you meet for the first time, or the urge to have lunch at an unfamiliar restaurant only to meet your future wife on her first day of work—these are all examples of absolute knowledge we experience in daily life.

When the master 77 is in lower throttle, which is most of the time, it downshifts to $7 + 7 = 1 \times 12 + 2 = 12/3$ of the catalyst (3) through new beginnings (1) of duality and balance (2). This is the steady and deliberate energy of allowing our intuition to guide us (3) to new experiences (1) of physical-spiritual knowing (2). However, when restricted or frustrated, the 77 can stray to the lower tendencies of the 12/3 vibration of being pushy, manipulative, and opinionated.

Example of Master 77

A person with the birth name *George Alexander Dale* would have a master 77 expression number: $(7 + 5 + 6 + 9 + 7 + 5) + (1 + 3 + 5 + 6 + 1 + 5 + 4 + 5 + 9) + (4 + 1 + 3 + 5) = (3 \times 12 + 3) + (3 \times 12 + 3) + (1 \times 12 + 1) =$ master 33 + master 33 + master 11 = master 77.

88 · Mastery of Manifestation

Unreduced Qualities: Absolute abundance

Reduced Qualities (of the 8 + 8 = 14/5): Freedom, growth, adaptability, trust, inner child

Negative Tendencies (of the 14/5): Restless, impatient, reactionary, domineering

What It Means When Master Number 88 Appears

The master 88 is the vibration of absolute abundance and instantaneous manifestation. We achieve the 88 energy in moments of feeling absolute abundance, such as when we meet the person of our dreams, conceive a child, or overcome a life-threatening illness.

Although rare, this energy can also occur in a person's birth name or formal title, such as that of Queen Elizabeth II, as shown in our example below. Her life is therefore a double-edged sword of being born into extreme wealth and privilege coupled with enormous responsibility to manifest abundance for an entire nation. This takes a special soul with a strength of character and unwavering sense of duty to incarnate into such a challenging role, characteristics that I believe Queen Elizabeth personifies with dignity and grace.

When the master 88 is in lower throttle, which is most of the time, it downshifts to 8 + 8 = 1x12 + 4 = 14/5 of change (5) through new beginnings (1) of structure and stability (4). This is an energy of adaptability in the face of change, a quality the queen also strives to embody. However, when restricted or frustrated, the 88 can stray to the lower tendencies of the 14/5 vibration of being restless, impatient, and reactionary and forcing order.

Example of Master 88

Her Royal Majesty Queen Elizabeth the Second of the United Kingdom, the formal title of the longest reigning British monarch in history: (8 + 5 + 9) + (9 + 6 + 7 + 1 + 3) + (4 + 1 + 1 + 5 + 1 + 2 + 7) + (8 + 3 + 5 + 5 + 5) + (5 + 3 + 9 + 8 + 1 + 2 + 5 + 2 + 8) + (2 + 8 + 5) + (1 + 5 + 3 + 6 + 5 + 4) +

$(6 + 6) + (2 + 8 + 5) + (3 + 5 + 9 + 2 + 5 + 4) + (2 + 9 + 5 + 7 + 4 + 6 + 4) = (1x12 + \underline{10}/1\underline{10}/\underline{11}) + (2x12 + 2/22) + (1x12 + 9/19/\underline{10}) + (2x12 + 2/22) + (3x12 + 7/37/\underline{10}) + (1x12 + 3/13/4) + (2x12 + 0/20/2) + (1x12 + 0/10/1) + (1x12 + 3/13/4) + (2x12 + 4/24/6) + (3x12 + 1/31/4) = \underline{11}$ + master 22 + $\underline{10}$ + master 22 + $\underline{10}$ + 4 + 2 + 1 + 4 + 6 + 4 = master 22 + master 22 + 4x12 + 4/master 44 = master 88.

99 · Mastery of Completion

Unreduced Qualities: Absolute acceptance

Reduced Qualities (of the 9 + 9 = 16/7): Knowledgeable, truthful, authentic, faithful

Negative Tendencies (of the 16/7): Pretentious, overanalytical, skeptical, fanatical, elitist

What It Means When Master Number 99 Appears

The master 99 is the vibration of absolute acceptance, of achieving a sense of complete peace and closure. We arrive at the 99 vibration when we reach a state of total acceptance, such as when we choose peace over war, find forgiveness for another who has wronged us, or find peace with ourselves in our final moments before passing.

When the master 99 is in lower throttle, which is most of the time, it downshifts to $9 + 9 = 1 \times 12 + 6 = 16/7$ of truth (7) through new beginnings (1) of love and harmony (6), a sense of spiritual peace that every ending is a new beginning for exploring love. However, when restricted or frustrated, the 99 can stray to the lower tendencies of the 16/7 vibration of being pretentious, overanalytical, skeptical, fanatical, and elitist.

Example of Master 99

In the year 117 CE (master 99 in base-12) the Roman Empire reached its peak under the reign of Emperor Trajan. Trajan's death that same year marked the end of the expansion of the Roman Empire (9). Trajan was born on a 9 month (September) and a 9 year (53 AD = $5 + 4 \times 12 + 5 = 45/9$) and his current name of *Emperor Trajan* had the 9 vibration: $(5 + 4 + 7 + 5 + 9 + 6 + 9) + (2 + 9 + 1 + 1 + 1 + 5) = (3 \times 12 + 9) + (1 \times 12 + 7) = 39/10/1 + 17/8 = 1 + 8 = 9$. As his third and final growth cycle (year of birth) was a 9, it was fitting that he completed his life path with his passing during that period at the 9 vibration age of 64 ($5 \times 12 + 4 = 54/9$).

<u>10 10</u> · Mastery of Awareness

Unreduced Qualities: Absolute awareness

Reduced Qualities (of the <u>10</u> + <u>10</u> = 18/9): Content, accepting, forgiving, selfless, grateful

Negative Tendencies (of the 18/9): Unfulfilled, defeated, vengeful, regretful, fatalistic

What It Means When Master Number <u>10 10</u> Appears

The master <u>10 10</u> is the vibration of absolute awareness, of profound clarity that sees the truth beyond the bias of our ego. We encounter the <u>10 10</u> energy when we experience a direct spiritual connection, such as when we have a lucid dream and communicate with a loved one who has passed, when we survive a near-death experience with expanded awareness, or when our psychic abilities open to the point that we can perceive spirit while consciously awake.

When the master <u>10 10</u> is in lower throttle, it downshifts to <u>10</u> + <u>10</u> = 1x12 + 8 = 18/9 of completion (9) through new beginnings (1) of manifestation and abundance (8). This is the sense of wholeness and comfort of knowing that every moment is a new opportunity to manifest abundance for ourselves and others. However, when restricted or frustrated, the <u>10 10</u> can stray to the lower tendencies of the 18/9 vibration of being unfulfilled and pessimistic.

Example of Master <u>10 10</u>

The term *quantum computer software technology*: $(8 + 3 + 1 + 5 + 2 + 3 + 4)$ $+ (3 + 6 + 4 + 7 + 3 + 2 + 5 + 9) + (1 + 6 + 6 + 2 + 5 + 1 + 9 + 5) + (2 + 5$ $+ 3 + 8 + 5 + 6 + 3 + 6 + 7 + 7) = (2x12 + 2) + (3x12 + 3) + (2x12 + \underline{11}) +$ $(4x12 + 4) = $ master 22 + master 33 + master 11 + master 44 = master <u>10 10</u>.

In the base-12 year of <u>10</u> <u>10</u> <u>10</u> (1570 in base-10), the first modern atlas of the world was published by cartographer Abraham Ortelius. In the base-12 year of 10 <u>10</u> <u>10</u> (1858 in base-10), ironically, Canada adopted the decimal (base-10) currency system!

<u>11</u> <u>11</u> · Mastery of Illumination

Unreduced Qualities: Absolute understanding

Reduced Qualities (of the <u>11</u> + <u>11</u> = 1<u>10/11</u>): Understanding, knowing, wise, inspired

Negative Tendencies (of the 1<u>10/11</u>): Oblivious, unreceptive, naïve, disillusioned, ignorant

What It Means When Master Number <u>11</u> <u>11</u> Appears

The master <u>11</u> <u>11</u> is the vibration of absolute understanding, of fully integrating the lessons revealed through the absolute awareness of the <u>10</u> <u>10</u>. We attain the <u>11</u> <u>11</u> energy when we have total understanding of our soul's evolution. This I believe can only be reached when we return to spirit and regain the full consciousness of our higher self or by the select few living spiritual masters who have achieved that level of enlightenment.

For the rest of us still walking the physical path, we can only experience mastery of illumination to the level of its lower octave of <u>11</u> <u>11</u> = 1x12 + <u>10</u> = 1<u>10/11</u> of personal illumination (<u>11</u>) through new beginnings (1) of awareness (<u>10</u>), an openness to learn. Yet when restricted or frustrated, the 1<u>10/11</u> can stray to its lower tendencies of being unreceptive, suspicious, and set in its ways.

Example of Master <u>11</u> <u>11</u>

Amongst students of metaphysics, the master number <u>11</u> <u>11</u> is symbolic of the current shift of humanity to higher consciousness (see "Harmonic Convergence of 11:11: Humanity Choosing Light Over Dark," on page 154). It often catches our attention as the recurring time of 11:11 on clocks and appropriately so. In terms of base-12 cycles, <u>11</u> full cycles (hours) plus 11 remainder (minutes) is precisely what the master number <u>11</u> <u>11</u> represents: <u>11</u> full octaves above the frequency of <u>11</u>. As such, clock time is a perfect tool for spirit to send us numerologically meaningful messages in base-12.

5

HOW BASE-12 NUMEROLOGY ILLUMINATES THE WAY

In the first part of the book, you learned the basics of base-12 numerology and how to prepare and interpret your own personal Base-12 Numerology Road Map. In this chapter, we broaden our view from the practical to the spiritual, the individual to the collective, and the finite to the timeless.

As the base-12 cycle of experience culminates with the enlightened frequency of the 11 of illumination, it is from this vantage point that we can understand the full cycle most clearly. And the best way to understand the nature of illumination is through the metaphor of light, a metaphor that will serve as our guide throughout this chapter.

We will illustrate the power of base-12 numerology for illuminating lessons through a couple of global events that affected all of humanity: the 9/11 terrorist attacks of 2001 and the cosmological event in 1987 known as the Harmonic Convergence. Major events such as these serve to highlight just how interconnected we are and how we hold the torch for each other as we find our way. We examine our role as torchbearers more deeply.

Next, we consider how our path as torchbearers is not linear and finite, as we are made to believe in physicality, but rather cyclical and eternal. Every experience is a round trip through the same base-12 cycle of themes, though always an opportunity to discover something new each time and to grow. Still, sometimes we get stuck in a repeating pattern that stalls our growth, so we discuss how this happens and how we can break free.

We then consider how paired themes in base-12 numerology add and subtract in meaningful ways. They can act as both mirrors and opposites depending on their relative position in the base-12 cycle, these relationships clearly portrayed in the geometry of the base-12 vibration itself.

Free of the illusion of time, we consider how everything happens now in the present moment. So how to be fully present in each moment is of vital importance. This we address through the context of numerology, including a strategy for avoiding the counterproductive trap of multitasking.

We conclude the chapter with the ultimate expression of the base-12 numerology cycle, reincarnation. This is the happy ending we always hoped for, that death is not the end but just a visit back home to spirit before our next big adventure.

Light as a Metaphor

I have been fascinated with light and color from an early age. I fondly recall my first and only science fair project as a young teen in which I demonstrated how a glass prism can separate white light into the colors of the rainbow and then recombine them back again into white light. I found it so magical how white light, though appearing so neutral and clear, actually consisted of a blended spectrum of vividly colored frequencies.

More than just a fundamental property of physics, the refraction of light serves as a powerful metaphor of unity through diversity and wholeness through inclusion. This metaphor has always stuck with me and was perhaps my first lesson in how the natural world informs and illuminates our human experience and that we all belong together, not apart.

The visible spectrum of light beautifully demonstrates how numerology works too since the full sequence of number energies add together in the same unifying way. The spectrum of colors in white light may be considered the spectrum of number frequencies from 1 to <u>10</u> in base-12. When added together, these combine to give the "white light" of the <u>11</u> energy of illumination.

$$1 + 2 + 3 + 4 + 5 + 6 + 7 + 8 + 9 + \underline{10} = 55 \text{ in base-10}$$
$$= 4 \times 12 + 7 = 47 \text{ in base-12}$$
$$= 4 + 7 = \underline{11}$$

Also, just as adding more white light to already white light does not change it, adding <u>11</u> to the sum of 1 to <u>10</u> doesn't alter the already "fully illuminated" numerological energy of the total.

$$1 + 2 + 3 + 4 + 5 + 6 + 7 + 8 + 9 + \underline{10} + \underline{11} = 66 \text{ in base-10}$$
$$= 5 \times 12 + 6 = 56 \text{ in base-12}$$
$$= 5 + 6 = \underline{11}$$

In this way, we see that numerology expresses the true nature of light perfectly as a harmonious blending of vibrational frequencies.

Let's now expand our light metaphor to better appreciate how events in our lives help illuminate fundamental spiritual truths about ourselves and our relationships with others. But how can moments of illumination bring clarity to our often confusing and chaotic lives?

It all comes down to an openness to learn. When we presume that we already know everything we need to know, we close ourselves off from evolving further. This only serves to make our lives more difficult, as a closed and unreceptive vibration attracts people and situations that reflect that same resistance. Conversely, when we have a desire to learn more about ourselves and others, we invite circumstances which facilitate that learning. We will still encounter events that take us by surprise, but we will be less distracted by the drama of others and more receptive to the underlying value of the message.

I also believe that the lessons of illumination we are meant to learn present themselves in a gentler way when we are already receptive to learning. The universe doesn't need to hit us on the head with a two-by-four if a gentle tap on the hand will do. In my own experience, many of the more dramatic lessons and uncomfortable bonks on the head I've encountered were only amplified because I was avoiding them out of fear. Those lessons I more courageously faced, on the other hand, inevitably turned out easier than expected.

Remember, the universe knows what it will take to teach us what we need to learn based on how easy or difficult we want to make it. My vote is to make life as easy as possible, so I try to remember that whenever I find myself digging in my heels and closing off my mind.

Illuminating Lessons for Humanity

We always remember those individuals who made a profound difference in our lives—mentors and teachers who helped illuminate the way for us at timely points in our journey. These include both inspirational role models and frustrating antagonists who broadened our understanding and challenged our perspective in some important way.

We likewise never forget those powerfully luminating events, events that snap us to attention and leave us forever changed. These include both personal moments of illumination that affect us individually and global events that affect all of humanity. The tragic events of September 11, 2001, are one such reminder of the illuminating power of the 11.

Terrorist Attacks of 9/11: Illumination of Duality

When we consider the base-12 numerology of that date, we find a profoundly accurate energetic description of the terrorist attacks that occurred that day and their global impact.

When added together as single digits, 9/11 (like the 911 emergency number it reflects) has the 9 + 1 + 1 = 11 vibration of "illumination," as does the eleventh day when viewed separately from the month. Likewise, if the 11 is not recognized as the single-digit lesson of illumination it was meant to be, it will be mistaken for two 1s, which represents the much lower vibration of the 1 + 1 = 2 of duality and polarity. This event therefore illuminated the extreme duality of which humanity is capable: the senseless violence and hatred that motivated the attacks and the global outpouring of compassion and unity galvanized in their aftermath. A lesson in dark and light that will never be forgotten.

Still, how each person or nation responded to the message varied greatly and does so to this day. Border security and immigration restrictions were heightened by many countries, with racial tensions worsening between those who resonated with the 2's duality energy of retaliation and fear. Others saw the event as the <u>11</u> of illumination, a wake-up call to work harder toward dissolving racial and religious barriers and to get to the root cause of the cultural fear and distrust. Still others took a stance somewhere in between.

This is another aspect of the <u>11</u> and of all multiple digit numbers: they have a complex vibration with a multilayered, multidimensional quality that speaks personally to each of us on multiple levels and at different times in our lives. Like the mirrored 1s of its numerical form, the <u>11</u> represents the individual looking at another and seeing themselves reflected back. To me, this applies to both the 1 of each of us as individuals and the 1 of humanity as a collective consciousness. As such, witnessing an event such as 9/11 causes us not only to look at our own personal safety, values, and morality, but also our connection to each other and to the greater good.

When we consider the 9 month and <u>11</u> day separately before adding together, we find further truth in that date. This event marked the tragic end (9) of many innocent lives, but also the illumination and realization (<u>11</u>) that countries and cultures cannot perpetuate such hatred any longer. Even in terms of the physical buildings targeted, the attack resulted in the destruction (9) of twin towers (<u>11</u>). Fittingly, those two towers symbolic of duality and separation were replaced by a single beautiful structure symbolic of unity and named One World Trade Center.

Further, the original twin towers were opened on a 1<u>11</u> date of April 4, 1973 (4 + 4 +1185 = 1x12 + <u>11</u> = 1<u>11</u>). Thus, their life began with an energy of new beginnings (1) of illumination (<u>11</u>) and ended with one of completion (9) of illumination (<u>11</u>). A humbling parallel with the illuminating role these buildings played and perhaps were always meant to play from their inception.

Last, the year of 2001 in base-12 is equal to 11<u>1</u>09 = 1x12 + 9 = 19/<u>10</u>, the energy of awareness and insight (10) through new beginnings (1) of completion (9). A poignant message of hope as we closed the door on a 2,000-year period of low-energy duality and began the new millennium with a heightened awareness.

Harmonic Convergence of 11:11:
Humanity Choosing Light Over Dark

Another potent example of the <u>11</u> as a marker of illumination for humanity was the 11:11 event known as the Harmonic Convergence. This event, which has both astrological and spiritual significance, occurred on August 17, 1987.

In terms of astrology, this event signified when the sun, moon, and six planets formed part of a *grand trine*, being aligned 120 degrees from each other at the apexes of an equilateral triangle. Also, during this event, the sun, moon, Mars, and Venus were all in direct alignment with each other, astrologically called a *conjunction*. Spiritually, the Harmonic Convergence is considered the decision point when the vibration of humanity's collective consciousness said yes to enlightenment and no to further separation and fear. This was the energetic tipping point where light and compassion exceeded darkness and fear.

Two things immediately caught my eye regarding the geometry of this alignment. First was the 120-degree equilateral triangle formation overall and, second, the direct alignment of the sun, moon, Mars, and Venus. The 120-degree grand trine arrangement matches the 120-degree phase shift of the two sine waves of the base-12 numerology vibration. Also, Mars symbolizes aggression and war, Venus love, the moon our unconscious, and the sun our consciousness. With their direct alignment, we can understand why this positional moment in our solar system projected an energy of a major decision point, when we would choose between love and war and to consciously acknowledge and release what we unconsciously fear.

When we look at the numerology of this pivotal date, we see its spiritual meaning precisely given. The year of 1987 equates to 1197 in base-12, which reduces to 1x12 + 6 = 16/7. This means spiritual truth (7) through the unity/

convergence (1) of harmony/love (6) or spiritual truth through harmonic convergence. Further, when we consider the full date of August 17, 1987, we obtain $8 + 15/6 + 1197/16/7 = 8 + 6 + 7 = 1x12 + 9 = 19/\underline{10}$ which means awareness (10) through new beginnings (1) of completion (9). The day of the Harmonic Convergence therefore marked that moment of awareness ($\underline{10}$) when we chose greater enlightenment over lower consciousness, while the year of 1987 energized that spiritual awareness (16/7) throughout the year.

In Lee Carroll's profoundly insightful channelings of the multidimensional consciousness known as *Kryon*, he mentions that the 11:11 event was later celebrated on January 11, 1992, as that specific date and the Harmonic Convergence of 1987 itself happened at the same time in an energetic way. This celebration was initiated by a channel named *Solara*, who received this spiritual insight through her own intuitive connection.

I never understood why Kryon claimed these dates were energetically the same until I applied base-12 numerology. In base-12, January 11, 1992 = 1 + $\underline{11}$ + 11$\underline{100}$ = 1+$\underline{11}$+10/1 = 1 + $\underline{11}$ + 1 or "11:11." Also note the six 1s in the base-12 date before being reduced. This also reveals how this date resonated with the harmony and love of the 6 through the convergence of six 1s, as did the year of 1987 with a vibration of 16/7.

It's also interesting to note that the sun has a consistent radiance cycle of solar activity of approximately eleven years. The next galactic harmonic event that Kryon informed us of was the *Harmonic Concordance* that occurred eleven years later on November 9, 2003. Not only did this date align with the eleven-year solar radiance cycle, but it also had the same 19/$\underline{10}$ vibration as that of the Harmonic Convergence (i.e., November 9, 2003 = $\underline{11}$ + 9 + 11$\underline{10}$ $\underline{11}$ = $\underline{11}$ + 9 + $\underline{11}$1/10/1 = 19/$\underline{10}$).

So, where the Harmonic Convergence was the convergence of the 1s of our illusion as separate individuals into the 6 of collective harmony and love, the Harmonic Concordance celebrated our passing of that marker on its first solar anniversary. I realized that my own spiritual awakening happened eleven years later upon the completion of the next solar cycle in 2014.

Holding the Torch for Others

We are constantly presented with opportunities to be the light for others—as a shoulder to lean on, a patient listener, a voice of reason, a positive example, or a friendly smile. It's a wonderful feeling to help raise the spirits (i.e., vibration) of others, though we are often surprised how little that takes. It's easy to question our worthiness as a role model for others, our ego trying to make us think less of ourselves. We tend to be hesitant to stand up for others for fear of exposing our own shortcomings.

Still, no one said we need to be perfect to spread light to others—quite the opposite. We are at our most authentic and perfectly flawed when we wear our strengths and weaknesses with pride. This makes us approachable and relatable to others, as anyone can see through false pride and inflated ego. Numerology lets us appreciate our strengths and weaknesses for the valuable assets they are, as powerful levers for learning and growth.

Returning to our analogy of light, we are at our best and most helpful when we openly share our full spectrum of experience, our own complement of colors regardless how developed or weak we believe our individual qualities to be. Again, the "white light" representing balanced enlightenment is the sum of all frequencies of light. We can do our part by sharing where we shine most brightly, while allowing others to do the same. We needn't try to be all things to all people but simply share our gifts wherever we are and with whomever we encounter. In this way we are lighthouses, continuously illuminating the way for anyone who comes near our little corner of the world.

This to me is the secret to holding the torch for others: sharing your gifts generously, whatever they may be, while allowing others to share theirs too. Compassion and kindness are brilliant lights indeed, so a little goes a long way. Through the lens of numerology, we can focus our light where it can do the most good.

Full Circle We Come

Reaching the <u>11</u> of illumination and returning home to the 0 of potential marks the completion of a full circuit of our vibrational journey through the twelve number energies of the base-12 cycle. In our normal linear perspective, we would consider each such cycle as an ending, a finish line crossed, an accomplishment. And it most definitely is, but so much more.

Living an intuitive, vibrationally aware, and authentic life means knowing there is no finish line, no end to our evolution and no limit to our potential for creativity and love. The base-12 cycle that reverberates throughout the cosmos and through every living cell and DNA molecule in our bodies is just that. It's a never-ending cycle of multidimensional discovery that repeats through every lifetime, every moment and every heart beat we experience. Each time we circumnavigate the cycle of 12, on any level, we learn more about our ourselves, each other, and why we're all in this together. We are like eternal voyagers, circling the same vibrational world of 12 many times, but each time attempting a different route through different weather conditions in order to discover something new.

Still, sometimes we get accustomed to a particular route and that becomes a repeating pattern in our life. This could be a repeating pattern of dysfunctional relationships, compulsive behaviors, chronic health issues, or any number of other signs that we're stuck in a vibrational groove. To break that pattern, we need to uncover what core belief we hold about ourselves that keeps attracting it to us. This belief often stems back to a fear we acquired in childhood and never fully released, such as the fear of abandonment, fear of lack, or low self-worth.

Whatever the cause, base-12 numerology teaches us that the fear to make any change means we are stuck somewhere between the 4 of structure and stability and the 5 of change. We are either fearful of leaving the safety, order and predictability of the 4 or fearful of stepping into the risk, disruption and uncertainty of the 5.

Still, we also know that it is the 6 of love that powers the 5 of change and enables us to take that leap of faith. So, whatever the blockage holding you back, shining love on the fear and holding compassion for yourself will help dissolve the impasse and give you the strength to boldly set a new course.

The Balancing Act of Mirror Images and Opposites

Now that we have explored the base-12 numerology cycle from many angles, we have a better understanding of what living a balanced and complete life really means. And when we stand back and consider the geometry of the base-12 vibration itself, we see how that balance is achieved: through the relationship between numbers as mirror-image reflections and opposites.

Each of the individual energies in the first half of the base-12 cycle from 1 to 5 have an enlightened higher-frequency reflection in the second half of the cycle from 7 to 11. Every pair of energies is a mirror image of each other in the overall base-12 waveform, always reflecting through the central 6 of love.

Each of these mirrored pairs represent complementary themes such that we need to understand the lower frequency energy to understand its more enlightened counterpart. We need to experience the 2 of duality of both polarities, for example, before we can understand the 10 of awareness that every vibration requires duality to exist.

Numerologically, mirrored pairs of themes always add together to the 12 (0) of cycle completion and potential (e.g., 2 + 10 = 12) and average together to the 6 of love (e.g., [2 + 10] / 2 = 12 / 2 = 6). This reveals the complementary nature of mirrored energies. Also, as these mirrored pairs always reflect through the 6 of love as the balance point of the overall cycle, it is therefore love that provides balance in all circumstances, whether in the form of self-love, love for another or compassion for all of humanity and the planet.

Each of the lower frequency themes likewise has a polarized counterpart within the higher frequency themes. This is easier to see when the cycle is viewed as a circle instead of a waveform.

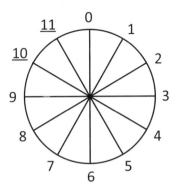

Polarized Frequency Pairs

This creates polarized pairs of energies, each pair being 180 degrees opposite each other, and is responsible for the vibrational tug-of-war we tend to experience with every situation we encounter. This concept we touched on earlier when we explained astrology and the relentless push/pull of opposing signs and planets. For instance, where the 2 of duality represents our personal struggle with not knowing our true physical-spiritual nature, the 8 of manifestation represents its energetic opposite, of knowing and embracing our physical-spiritual duality in service to others. Numerologically, polarized pairs of energy always subtract to the 6 of love (e.g., 8 − 2 = 6), illustrating how polarity fundamentally means the difference between love and the lack of love.

So, where mirrored pairs are complements, polarized pairs are opposites. And together they provide us with a powerful strategy for understanding how energy really works and what makes us tick—and pop a gear once in a while!

In short, the often confusing and stressful emotions we feel and that play out around us always come down to energies being out of balance. Through our understanding of the base-12 cycle and how balance is achieved through mirrored and polarized energies, we can learn how to neutralize the root causes of stress and to master our vibrational lives. Others can't help but notice the new "balanced you" because your dominant vibration becomes the 6 of love and harmony, the natural universal vibration to which we all gravitate.

The Infinite Now

We as humans are the only species on earth possessing the power of conscious choice and self-awareness but also the only species that goes against its own best interests by attempting to do too many things at once. We didn't start out that way in the wild but have acquired that counterproductive behavior since.

We are conditioned throughout our lives by society and our own ego to push more, achieve more and fret that we're running out of time to accomplish it all. We clog our minds with the constant worry of conflicting priorities and looming deadlines, reducing our effectiveness with the one thing we should be focusing on at any given time.

When we multitask, we are essentially trying to vibrationally juggle many balls in the numerological cycle at once. This only lessens our performance overall and wastes the opportunity for mastery in any one task. As mastery of energetic themes in a focused sequential progression is the essence of numerology and of the soul's evolution itself, multitasking works against our very spiritual progress.

Still, it's amazing how well the human mind can focus once we do manage to shut out everything else other than the current moment. I am sure you have experienced that state of deep concentration and relaxed flow many times. Maybe it's when you were so engaged in a sport or hobby that time seemed to stand still, or when you were so absorbed by a deeply fulfilling project at work or so engrossed in a novel or movie that you felt part of it. It is when we are singularly engaged in a passion that we experience these peak moments of joy, not when our attention is divided.

Numerology is a wonderful tool for teaching us how to focus in the moment because it helps us dig deeply into individual energetic themes. And as discussed previously, how thoroughly we experience each stage of the base-12 cycle determines how vibrationally balanced we are as we move on to the next. The eternal journey of our soul truly is an infinite series of many "now" moments and living each moment as if it were the only one (because it is) is how we can recalibrate our spiritual focus.

So, the next time you feel overwhelmed with too much to do, pick the one thing you feel most drawn to (or least opposed to) in that moment and give it your full attention. Dedicating some time to this one task will put you back onto your path of resonance and will guide you to the next most appealing and therefore most appropriate task. Following your intuitive compass in this way brings a flow and appreciation to even the most mundane of activities. And the flow you will be feeling will be the natural momentum of the base-12 cycle carrying you forward.

The Base-12 Reincarnation Cycle

From our limited perspective of the daily game of life, we now expand our view to the reincarnation cycle through which we strive to master that game. This is the spiritual training ground of our higher self and the truth behind the veil of physicality.

Each physical incarnation is an energetic game board we set up for ourselves to experience certain themes and learn certain lessons. Although the rules of the game and the layout of the board remain the same in the form of the base-12 numerology cycle, we can play each round any way we wish. Our objective is vibrationally set by the numerology of our birth date. We then select a game piece and starting position that suits the way we want to play. This selection is made through our birth name. Together, our birth date and name determine our Base-12 Numerology Road Map for each round of the game.

Now, an important rule to the game is that we begin each round with intentional amnesia of our true eternal nature. This ensures that we take the game seriously and explore each life as if it were our only one. In terms of the base-12 numerology cycle, this amnesia happens once we leave the 0 of the spiritual plane and step into the 1 of physicality. As revealed by the geometry of the base-12 waveform, it is at 1 that we first touch the horizontal "reality" axis and at <u>11</u> where we touch it last. Between 1 and <u>11</u> then is where we negotiate the vibrational obstacle course called life, largely unaware of who we really are.

When we've finished exploring our road map, we say farewell to our physical vehicle at <u>11</u> and return home to 0. In that instant, the forgotten knowledge of our true spiritual nature returns to us in full.

Everything we are and everything above and below us can be thought of as an infinite progression of base-12 vibrational cycles, all nested within each other and interconnected as one. All That Is/Source/God is the all-encompassing vibration within which all other cycles are expressed including humanity's spiritual evolution through the collective evolution of all souls, each soul's spiritual growth through countless physical incarnations, the life path we navigate within each incarnation, the many events and relationships we experience within each lifetime and the various themes we explore within each experience.

Thus, we conclude this chapter by dispelling perhaps our greatest fear of all, death. Once we acknowledge physical death as simply our return back home and to our true essence as spiritual consciousness, it suddenly becomes a welcome back party. A chance to reconnect with our soul family in spirit, to review and integrate everything we learned, and to plan our next exciting road trip.

Of course, we may choose to remain in spirit awhile to study new areas that fascinate us or to serve as guides for others. The choice is ours, but whatever we choose will always be for the highest good and always based in love. Because that's what we are—love, expressed in wonderfully unique ways through the base-12 language of numerology.

SAMPLE PROFILES
AND WORD MEANINGS

I am always amazed at how accurately base-12 numerology reflects one's life path and means of expression, including famous personalities. Following are fourteen big names you have no doubt heard of, along with their life paths (overall life theme and lessons to learn) and expression numbers (general direction, talents and potential).

Celebrity readings are fun to explore as they provide insight into the fascinating lives these people live, but they also remind us that we are all painted from the same vibrational palette of energies. We've just chosen different roles to play this time around.

Sample Profiles of Famous People

Oprah Gail Winfrey (birth name: Orpah Gail Winfrey)

Born January 29, 1954

Life Path = 1 29 1954 (base-10) = 1 + 25/7 + 116<u>10</u>/16/7 (base-12) = 1 + 7 + 7 = **13/4**

Expression = 69718 7193 5956957 = 27/9 + 18/9 + 3<u>10</u>/11 = 9 + 9 + 11 = **27/9**

Oprah's life path is to learn about structure and stability (4) through new beginnings (1) of the catalyst (3). She experienced both sides of this influential 3 vibration in seeking stability for herself. On the negative side, she was abused as a child, was raised in three different family circumstances between her mother, father, and grandmother, and faced sexist and racial stereotyping in a male-dominated media industry. On the positive side, she has applied these lessons very constructively in creating stability and structure for herself and others (4) through new beginnings (1) of personal empowerment and self-improvement (3). And she does so with global reach.

Her three growth cycles were to experience independence or isolation (1) in her youth, gain spiritual knowledge (7) through the duality (2) of change (5) in her main working years and then to advance that spiritual knowledge (7) through new beginnings (1) of love and harmony (6) for the balance of her life. Her experiences of sexual abuse and isolation as child (1), reinventing herself professionally and spiritually in adulthood (25/7) and further expanding her spiritual maturity and compassion ever since (16/7) align precisely with her intended path.

Oprah's expression number of 27/9 reveals her to be a humanitarian who is able to achieve completion and closure (9) through the duality (2) of spiritual truth and knowledge (7). Thus, her main direction and calling has been to help others reach a sense of completeness (9) by exploring the physical-spiritual duality (2) of their truth (7). She has most definitely achieved this and continues to do so through her informative and enlightening media programs and her generous philanthropy to many charitable causes.

Barack Hussein Obama II

Born August 4, 1961

Life Path = 8 4 1961 (base-10) = 8 + 4 + 1175/12/3 (base-12) = 8 + 4 + 3 = **13/4**

Expression = 219132 8311595 62141 = 16/7 + 28/$\underline{10}$ + 12/3 = 7 + $\underline{10}$ + 3 = **18/9**

Barack's life path is the same as Oprah's, to learn about structure and stability (4) through new beginnings (1) of the catalyst (3). However, he approached this differently in that his three growth cycles were to first explore practical manifestation and physical-spiritual balance (8) in his youth, stability and responsibility (4) in his main working years, and then catalytic influences (3) from that point forward.

Within his first growth cycle, he achieved abundance (8) for himself and others, excelling in school and pursuing civil rights. After graduating from Columbia University, he worked as a community organizer in Chicago before attending Harvard Law School. During his second growth cycle, he explored structure and stability (4), first as a civil rights attorney and professor of constitutional law and then as a senator before winning the presidency in 2009 and securing two terms. In his third growth cycle, which begins in 2020, he will no doubt continue to broaden his impact as an influential and eloquent catalyst (3) for humanitarian values.

It was during the 4 theme of his current growth cycle that he became the forty-fourth president (and first African American president) of the United States and the fourth US president to be awarded a Nobel Peace Prize for his efforts toward improving international diplomacy.

Barack's expression number of 18/9 once again shares the same outer 9 vibration as Oprah Winfrey's 27/9 expression number, though expressed through a different pair of inner energies. The 18/9 theme indicates that his main direction and calling is as a humanitarian who seeks completion (9) by creating new beginnings (1) of manifestation and abundance (8).

Barack exemplifies these qualities as a man of high integrity and social conscience (9) who through drive, leadership, and inspiration (1) strives to create abundance and equality for others (8).

Donald John Trump

Born June 14, 1946

Life Path = 6 14 1946 (base-10) = 6 + 12/3 + 1162/$\underline{10}$ (base-12) = 6 + 3 + $\underline{10}$ = **17/8**

Expression = 465134 1685 29347 = 1$\underline{11}$/10/1 + 18/9 + 21/3 = 1 + 9 + 3 = **master 11**

Donald's life path is all about exploring manifestation and abundance (8) through new beginnings (1) of spiritual truth and knowledge (7). His primary focus for exploring this theme thus far has been through business and financial abundance, an area in which he excels. His role as the president of the United States has provided him the opportunity to broaden his perspective regarding abundance from the financial to the humanitarian and from the individual and national to the global.

His three growth cycles have been to explore love and harmony (6) in his youth, the catalyst (3) through new beginnings (1) of duality (2) during his main working years and awareness and insight (<u>10</u>) in the remainder of his life. He had a stable, privileged, and comfortable (6) youth. In his mid-adult years, he experienced substantial duality both in the positive sense in the form of many lucrative deals and in the negative sense in the form of conflict in his business life with six bankruptcies and in his personal life being married three times. His third and current growth cycle has required him to expand his awareness (<u>10</u>) beyond himself at the same time that global scrutiny increases toward him.

Donald's powerful expression number of the master number 11 indicates that his calling and persona is self-mastery at best (11) and conflict and competitiveness at worst (1 + 1 = 2). We see this clearly, both in his strong self-confidence and resilience and his aggressive personal style, confrontational business approach and need to get his way. The 11 expression number at its most extreme is to cause conflict and polarity (2) through sheer force (1) of ego and self-interest (1). Still, like Oprah Winfrey and Barack Obama, he is living up to his expression number very faithfully though at opposite ends of the vibrational spectrum.

Diana Frances Spencer

Born July 1, 1961

Life Path = 7 1 1961 (base-10) = 7 + 1 + 1175/12/3 (base-12) = 7 + 1 + 3 =

11

Expression = 49151 6915351 1755359 = 18/9+26/8+2<u>11</u>/11 = 9+8+11 =

26/8

Diana's life path was the <u>11</u> of illumination, to illuminate truth. This was evident in her personal mission to support many humanitarian causes, but even more so in the light she shed on issues of personal privacy, media ethics, and class distinction through her challenges as part of the royal family. She was under constant scrutiny by the press and the monarchy with her troubled marriage and subsequent relationships on public display.

Having an <u>11</u> life path also meant she was prone to the <u>11</u>'s lower tendencies of being very independent, defiant, and disillusioned when unfulfilled. Her death in 1997 in a car crash while being pursued by paparazzi was a global moment of illumination that will never be forgotten. Still, her power to illuminate goodness lives on today in the fine example of her two well-adjusted sons who embody her personal charm and sincerity.

Her expression number of the 26/8 reveals her to be a seeker of abundance (8) through the duality (2) of love and harmony (6). This gave her the calling and disposition to persevere in manifesting something good (8) out of conflicted situations (2) lacking love and harmony (6). However, it also presented her with the double-edged sword of being a very private person with tremendous public popularity.

Her karmic lessons (letter energies missing from her name) of the 2 of duality and the 8 of manifesting abundance highlight that she didn't seek an easy path in exploring her 26/8 expression number. She made these her main vibrational weaknesses so that she could experience them deeply. With the 2 and the 8 as her chosen weaknesses, the 6 of love and harmony became the one aspect of her 26/8 expression number that could shine through most freely in her persona.

Steven Paul Jobs

Born February 24, 1955

Life Path = 2 24 1955 (base-10) = 2 + 20/2 + 116<u>11</u>/17/8 (base-12) = 2 + 2 + 8 = **10/1**

Expression = 125455 7133 1621 = 1<u>10</u>/<u>11</u> + 12/3 + <u>10</u> = <u>11</u> + 3 + <u>10</u> = **20/2**

Steve's life path is the 10/1 of exploring independence and new beginnings (1) through new beginnings (1) of potential (0). This accurately describes his meteoric life as a maverick innovator and gutsy business icon, building Apple into a high-tech powerhouse. As the name of his company had the same 10/1 vibration as his own personal life path (Apple = 1 + 7 + 7 + 3 + 5 = 1x12 + <u>11</u> = 1<u>11</u>/10/1), Apple was truly his life's work and synonymous with his identity.

His 10/1 life path also brought challenges of isolation, starting over, and fierce independence (1). He was put up for adoption by his parents at birth, dropped out of college in his first year, was forced out of Apple in 1985 by a power struggle, only to rejoin the near-bankrupt company in 1997 to bring it back to life. He was diagnosed with pancreatic cancer in 2003, a 10/1 year matching his life path (11<u>10</u> <u>11</u> = 1x12 + <u>11</u> = 1<u>11</u>/10/1).

His expression number of 20/2 reveals a direction and potential similar to Donald Trump's drive to compete and to stand out (11) but to explore that duality (2) through the pursuit of human and technological potential (20). This he pursued with passion and inspiration, while also experiencing the same negative potential of the 2 of impatience and conflict as often exemplified by Donald Trump.

Steve Jobs died on October 5, 2011 (<u>10</u> + 5 + 11<u>11</u>7/1x12 + 8/18/9 = <u>10</u> + 5 + 9 = 2x12 + 0 = 20/2). Not only was 2011 appropriately an 18/9 year of completion (9) through new beginnings (1) of abundance (8), but this specific date also matched his expression number of 20/2. Thus, the timing of his transition marked the completion of a life fully expressed, a completion through which he could now explore duality in terms of his physical-spiritual duality.

Marie Curie (birth name: Maria Salomea Skłodowska)

Born November 7, 1867

Life Path = 11 7 1867 (base-10) = $\underline{11}$+7+10$\underline{11}$7/17/8 (base-12) = $\underline{11}$+7+8

  = **master 22**

Expression = 41991 1136451 1236465121 = 20/2+19/$\underline{10}$+27/9 = 2+$\underline{10}$+9

  = **19/$\underline{10}$**

Marie Curie's life path was the powerful 22 of mastery of duality and the practical visionary. She explored this theme in all areas of her life. She is best known for her discovery of radiation and developing medical X-ray imaging and was not only the first woman to win a Nobel Prize, but also the first person to win twice and in two different sciences, physics and chemistry. She was born in Poland but became a French citizen, and her mother and eldest sister died when she was a child. She had two children of her own with her husband Pierre, a highly accomplished physicist like herself, and together they codiscovered the two elements of radium and polonium.

Note the prevalence of the number 2 in her life. She embodied her 22 life path masterfully indeed. Interestingly, the vibration of her husband's name, Pierre, (7 + 9 + 5 + 9 + 9 + 5 = 3x12 + 8 = 38/$\underline{11}$ in base-12) was the $\underline{11}$ of illumination and thus matched the vibration of the growth cycle Marie was in at the time they met. This resonance helped ensure they would be together, as did the vibration of Marie's age of 28 when they were married, being the 6 of love (28 = 2x12 + 4 = 24/6).

She followed the themes of her three growth cycles perfectly as well: the $\underline{11}$ of illumination, the 7 of spiritual truth and knowledge, and the 8 of manifestation and abundance. She was fascinated with the sciences and higher learning ($\underline{11}$) from an early age, she dedicated her working years to the advancement of knowledge and scientific truth (7), and by the end of her life she had achieved an amazing legacy of accomplishment (8).

Marie's expression number was the 19/$\underline{10}$ of awareness ($\underline{10}$) through new beginnings (1) of completion (9). This led her to her calling of discovering deep insights (10) regarding radiation as revolutionary treatment (1) for killing damaged cells such as cancer (9). With the 1 energy occurring eight times in the letters of her name, this was her karmic strength giving her the independence, drive, and innovation needed to achieve her ground-breaking role.

Her 19/10 expression number also revealed the profound sacrifice she was willing to make of gaining new insights for humanity (10) at the cost of exposing herself (1) to lethal amounts of radiation (9). She died of cancer in 1934, which was a 9 year of completion (1152 in base-12 = 1 + 1 + 5 + 2 = 9) and at the age of 66, which was an 11 year of illumination and learning complete (56 in base-12 = 5 + 6 = 11).

Albert Einstein

Born March 14, 1879

Life Path = 3 14 1879 (base-10) = 3 + 12/3 + 1107/9 (base-12) = 3 + 3 + 9
= **13/4**

Expression = 132592 59512595 = 110/11 + 35/8 = 11 + 8 = **17/8**

Albert's life path of 13/4 was the same challenging calling as Oprah Winfrey's and Barack Obama's: to learn about structure and stability (4) through new beginnings (1) of the catalyst (3). His chosen progression, however, was to have a catalytic youth (3), a catalytic career (3) through new beginnings (1) of duality (2,) and a humanitarian focus (9) for the balance of his life.

It is quite profound that his life path of 13/4 played out both as an innovative catalyst for redefining our understanding of the structure (4) of the universe, but also as the unwitting catalyst (3) for the development of the atomic bomb. This no doubt heightened his humanitarian resolve (9) to use knowledge and technology for good instead of evil.

His 17/8 expression number indicates his calling was to manifest abundance (8) through new beginnings (1) of truth and knowledge (7). Einstein's ground-breaking theories of how the universe manifests (8) completely redefined (1) our understanding (7) of the cosmos, thus fulfilling his calling profoundly. With five 5s in his name, the 5 energy of change, exploration, and courage was a particular strength that helped propel his insatiable curiousity forward. Still, this also made him very restless by nature, never content to rest on his laurels.

Stephen William Hawking

Born January 8, 1942

Life Path = 1 8 1942 (base-10) = 1 + 8 + 11$\underline{10}$/15/6 (base-12) = 1 + 8 + 6

= **13/4**

Expression = 1257855 5933914 8152957 = 29/$\underline{11}$ + 2$\underline{10}$/10/1 + 31/4 = $\underline{11}$

+ 1 + 4 = **14/5**

Stephen's life path of 13/4 is once again that of the pioneering (1) catalyst (3) of structure and stability (4) as shared by Albert Einstein, Oprah Winfrey, and Barack Obama. His three growth stages began as an independent, inventive, and driven (1) youth, followed by the prolific manifestation and abundance (8) from his thirties to late fifties, concluded by his later years of exploring love and harmony (6) through new beginnings (1) of change (5).

Like Einstein, Hawking's 13/4 life path drew him to explore the structure (4) of the cosmos and to elevate our understanding of physics, including his particularly influential (3) proof of the existence of black holes.

His expression number of 14/5 reveals a man who personified a profound ability to adapt and change (5) through new beginnings (1) of structure and stability (4), both in terms of rethinking the very foundation of physics and coura-geously dealing with his debilitating physical illness of ALS. Even the numerology of his illness (ALS = 1 + 3 + 1 = 5) matches the 5 vibration of his expression number and of the immobilizing nature of the disease itself.

Fascinating synchronicities surround Hawking's numerology. He was born on the three hundredth anniversary of the death of Galileo Galilei, the father of modern physics, and died on the anniversary of the birth of Einstein, with whom he shares the same 13/4 life path. The anniversary of Hawking's passing of March 14 is also Pi Day, on which we celebrate the famous mathematical ra-tio 3.14159... for the circle, while the specific date of March 14, 2018, has the illumination energy of the $\underline{11}$.

Ellen Lee DeGeneres

Born January 26, 1958

Life Path = 1 26 1958 (base-10) = $1 + 22 + 1172/\underline{11}$ (base-12) = $1 + 22 + \underline{11}$
   = **32/5**

Expression = 53355 355 457555951 = $19/\underline{10} + 11 + 3\underline{10}/11 = \underline{10} + 11 + 11$
   = **30/3**

Ellen's life path is to explore the 32/5 of change (5) through catalysts (3) of duality (2). This she has done profoundly in both her professional career as a comic, TV host, actress, and producer and in her personal life as openly gay advocate for the LGBT community. Major milestones in her journey of change occurred in years that had the 15/6 vibration of spreading love (6) through new beginnings (1) of change (5). This included her break-out appearance as a comic on *The Tonight Show Starring Johnny Carson* in 1986 (1196 in base-12 = 1x12 + 5 = 15/6), coming out as gay in an appearance on *The Oprah Winfrey Show* in 1997 (11\underline{10}5 in base-12 = 1x12 + 5 = 15/6) and marrying her longtime girlfriend Portia de Rossi in 2008 (11\underline{11}4 in based-12 = 1x12 + 5 = 15/6).

Her three growth cycles reveal just how big a mark she wanted to make in this life. Her first cycle was the independent 1 of new beginnings, her second cycle the master number 22 of the practical visionary, and her third cycle the inspirational \underline{11} of illumination.

Ellen's expression number is the 30/3 of the catalyst (3) through catalysts (3) of potential (0). This supports her 32/5 life path perfectly, giving her a gift for communication, creativity, and influence (3) and doing so by helping others (3) realize their unlimited potential (0). The three individual names in her birth name have enlightened vibrations even on their own, *Ellen* with the \underline{10} of awareness and insight, *Lee* with the master 11 of self-mastery, and *DeGeneres* also with the master 11 vibe.

It's interesting to note that her karmic strength (the most frequently occurring energy in the letters of her name) is 5, just like her life path. This energy occurs an impressive ten times. This makes her extremely courageous and adventurous, fun-loving, full of energy, and naturally witty. As her greatest strength matches her life path theme, she is vibrationally very well prepared to dive into her purpose deeply and fully.

Nikola Tesla

Born July 10, 1856

Life Path = 7 10 1856 (base-10) = 7 + <u>10</u> + 10<u>1</u>08/17/8 (base-12) = 7 + <u>10</u> + 8 = **21/3**

Expression = 592631 25131 = 22 +10/1 = **23/5**

Nikola's life path of 21/3 was to be a catalyst (3) through the duality (2) of independence and innovation (1). This is the signature of the brilliant inventor who advanced our understanding of electricity, including inventing alternating current, which is the energetic waveform of polarity itself (2).

His three growth stages were as a very spiritual and intellectual youth (7), a highly intuitive and perceptive inventor in his prime adult years (<u>10</u>), and then a wise visionary later in life who channeled his strong spiritual conviction and quest for knowledge into manifesting a lasting legacy of technical understanding (17/8). Interestingly, Donald Trump's life path of 17/8 matches Tesla's third growth stage.

His expression number of 23/5 revealed him to be a change agent whose drive never rested (5), despite constant conflict and opposition to his ideas (2) by influential people and circumstances (3). This included a life fraught with deep personal and emotional struggles and business challenges that eventually led to Nikola being penniless and alone in his old age.

Tesla is a classic example of an intensely focused and polarized personality, capable of great perseverance and accomplishment and equally dramatic hardship.

We can peer even further into Tesla's destiny as a technical powerhouse by looking at the numerology of his two names that added together to give his expression number of 23/5. His first name, *Nikola*, had the master number 22 vibration of mastery of duality of the master builder and practical visionary, while his last name, *Tesla*, resonated with the 10/1 of the pioneer (1) of new beginnings (1) of potential (0).

Elon Reeve Musk

Born June 28, 1971

Life Path = 6 28 1971 (base-10) = 6 + 24/6 + 1183/11 (base-12) = 6 + 6 +
   11 = **21/3**

Expression = 5365 95545 4312 = 17/8 + 24/6 + <u>10</u> = 8 + 6 + <u>10</u> = **20/2**

It's fascinating that Elon, one of the founders and current CEO of Tesla Inc., has the same influential life path of 21/3 as Nikola Tesla, for whom his company is named. Elon's inner energies, like Tesla's, are all about the duality (2) of new beginnings (1), of bringing ideas and people together in innovative ways while experiencing great opposition and challenge to making that happen.

His expression number of 20/2 reveals him to be a gifted collaborator, team builder, and negotiator, facilitating the 2 inner energy of his 21/3 life path. Where the inner energies of his life path teach him about the duality (2) of being an innovator (1), the inner energies of his expression number gives him the tools to explore that duality (2) through the unlimited potential (0) of pursuing his dreams. This likewise makes him prone to be an impractical idealist (0) and subject to inner conflict and self-doubt (2) when his dreams elude him. Nevertheless, like Einstein, Musk's name features five 5s and therefore the same adventurous spirit to persevere against all odds.

Also, Elon's first two growth cycles were to explore the 6 of harmony and love as part of his life path of mastering duality. This is evidenced by Elon being bullied throughout childhood, his parents divorcing when he was 9, and Elon experiencing three divorces of his own and the near bankruptcy in 2008 of his two companies, Tesla Motors Inc. and SpaceX. Sure enough, 2008 was a 6 year in base-12, thus amplifying lessons concerning love, self-love, harmony, and the lack thereof.

Elon's third growth cycle, which begins when he is 60, will explore the 11 theme of self-mastery. Through his earlier hard-fought lessons concerning harmony (6), this latter part of his life will focus on integrating those lessons into the wise, intuitive, and inspirational role model of the master 11.

Jane Goodall (birth name: Valerie Jane Morris-Goodall)

Born April 3, 1934

Life Path = 4 3 1934 (base-10) = 4 + 3+ 1152/9 (base-12) = 4 + 3 + 9 = **14/5**

Expression = 4135995 1155 469991 7664133 = 30/3 + 10/1 + 32/5 + 26/8 = 3 + 1 + 5 + 8 = **15/6**

Jane Goodall's life path has been to explore change (5) through new beginnings (1) of structure and stability (4). This describes her path well as the world's foremost expert of chimpanzees and a courageous activist (5) who became a pioneer (1) in protecting chimpanzees and their natural habitat (4).

Her work as a primatologist followed the themes of her three growth cycles faithfully: independence and drive (1) to study primates in Africa through early adulthood, becoming a force for changing attitudes (3) toward primates by her mid-adult years, then broadening her impact from that point onward as a vocal advocate for putting an end (9) to poaching, wild animal captivity, and other forms of cruelty.

Jane's expression number of 15/6 reveals her authentic calling and talents are for creating love and harmony (6) through new beginnings (1) of change (5). This dovetails well with her life path, which is all about mastering change (5).

It also mirrors her particular field of interest of observing the social dynamics and family bonds (6) between chimps and actually enables her to do so up close. Having a 6 expression number means that her outer personal vibration is that of the most fundamental frequency of nature, the 6 of love. The chimps she studied would have immediately sensed this and accepted her more readily into their midst because of it, rather than being perceived as a threat.

It's appropriate too that the word *chimpanzee* has the <u>11</u> vibration of illumination (3894715855 = 4x12 + 7 = 4 + 7 = <u>11</u>). This is so fitting both in terms of illuminating Jane Goodall's calling and highlighting our kinship with our wild ancestors.

Justin Drew Bieber

Born March 1, 1994

Life Path = 3 1 1994 (base-10) = 3 + 1 + 11102/12/3 (base-12) = 3 + 1 + 3
    = 7

Expression = 131295 4955 295259 = 19/10 + 111/10/1 + 28/10 = 10 + 1 +
    10 = 19/10

Justin's life path is to explore the theme of truth and knowledge (7). This put him on a journey of self-discovery and learning the truth of things, both in terms of finding his authentic self and discerning the integrity (or lack thereof) of others.

As a high-profile singer, songwriter, and actor from an early age, he was immersed in the demanding cut-throat world of the music business in which he had to grow up fast. His life path being the 7 directly (rather than indirectly through the reduction of a larger number, such as 16 = 1 + 6 = 7) reflects the intense life of learning he intended for himself. As he gains life experience, his outer focus on the 7 of practical life skills and street smarts will shift toward the higher expression of the 7 life path, the inner pursuit of spiritual truth.

Justin's three growth cycles are to experience the 3 theme of the catalyst in his youth, experience the 1 theme of new beginnings in his main working years, and then to reexamine the catalytic 3 theme for the balance of his life. His first growth cycle was very catalytic, as he was born to a single mother in Stratford, Ontario, and discovered by a talent scout at the young age of thirteen.

Interestingly, the numerology of his hometown, Stratford, matches his life path vibration of 7 (129126694 = 34/7). This therefore provided an energetically favorable environment for his talents to emerge quickly. He became a pop music sensation in his teen years, becoming an influential catalyst for his many adoring fans.

Upon completion of his first growth cycle at age twenty-nine, Justin will explore his second growth cycle and the theme of new beginnings (1) through age fifty-six. This will be a very regenerative period for him as he rediscovers himself personally and spiritually and explores an opportunity to take charge of his life after being heavily managed and influenced by others during his catalytic first growth cycle.

In his third growth cycle starting at age fifty-seven, Justin will return to the theme of the catalyst (3). However, now with the benefit of greater maturity and finding himself during his second growth cycle, this third and final cycle will expand his influence as a positive catalyst beyond just music.

Justin's expression number of 19/10 reveals him to be very aware and perceptive (10) with a natural drive and initiative (1) for following through on his goals (9). This perseverance and resilience enables him to brush himself off and start over when necessary (1) but can also make him quite obsessive and demanding in getting his way (9). The hyperaware 19/10 energy is also predisposed to becoming overwhelmed and to depression as the negative tendency of the 19 energy is a fear (1) of failure (9).

Even the titles of his albums reflect his 19/10 calling as an independent and driven seeker of truth on a 7 life path of spiritual awareness: *My World, Never Say Never, Believe, Journals,* and *Purpose.*

Jennifer Shrader Lawrence

Born August 15, 1990

Life Path = 8 15 1990 (base-10) = 8 + 13/4 + 11910/19/10 (base-12) = 8 + 4 + 10 = 110/11

Expression = 15559659 1891459 31595535 = 39/10/1 + 31/4 + 30/3 = 1 + 4 + 3 = 8

Jennifer's life path is to explore the 11 theme of illumination (11) through new beginnings (1) of awareness (10). This set her on a course to illuminate truth in her own life and on behalf of the greater good and to do so by bringing awareness to worthy causes.

This is the same 11 life path as Lady Diana Spencer, with both women being outspoken advocates of many humanitarian causes and both having a strong personal spirituality. An 11 life path also meant she was prone to the

<u>11</u>'s lower tendencies of being very independent and disillusioned when feeling unfulfilled.

Jennifer's three growth cycles are to experience the 8 theme of manifestation and abundance in her youth and early adulthood (to age twenty-five), the 4 of structure and stability in her main working years (to age fifty-two) and then the 19/<u>10</u> of awareness (<u>10</u>) through new beginnings (1) of completion (9) for the rest of her life.

In her first growth cycle, Jennifer learned about manifesting abundance (8) which she did very successfully. Like Justin Bieber, Jennifer Lawrence was discovered by a talent scout in her early teens and her acting career took off quickly.

She recently began her second growth cycle with a focus on exploring structure and stability (4). This will therefore be a period in which she gains a deeper understanding of structure versus instability and examine ways in which she can contribute to greater organization and order in her life and to the causes she supports.

In her third growth cycle, Jennifer will focus on the 19/<u>10</u> theme of awareness (<u>10</u>) through new beginnings (1) of completion (9). This will enable her to gain greater mastery of championing initiatives from start (1) to finish (9) to help bring greater awareness to issues she feels strongly about (<u>10</u>) .

Jennifer's expression number is the 8 of manifestation and abundance. Creating abundance for herself and others is therefore her greatest calling and that which best expresses her talents. As her first growth cycle was also the 8, it's not surprising that her natural acting ability was recognized from an early age and brought rapid fame and fortune.

Like Ellen DeGeneres, who has the 5 energy of change occurring ten times in her birth name, the 5 appears nine times in Jennifer's name. These two women therefore share the 5 energy as a core strength, or hidden passion, which includes a high level of energy, courage, and action. This would have contributed to her experiencing hyperactivity and social anxiety as a child and to her strong support in adulthood for equal rights for women and Planned Parenthood.

Another strength of Jennifer's is the 9 energy of completion, occurring five times in her name. This indicates a very dedicated, conscientious, and humanitarian vibe evidenced by her founding of the Jennifer Lawrence Foundation in support of children's needs and the arts.

The Prevalence of 1, 2, and 3 in the Numerology of High Achievers

In these sample profiles, you may have noticed the prevalence of the numbers 1, 2, and 3. This should come as no surprise as individuals with very ambitious life paths such as these tend to share these fundamental traits: the drive, originality, and leadership of the independent 1; the judgment, resilience, and personal magnetism of the polarized 2; and the creativity, communication skills, and influential presence of the catalytic 3.

This follows from our earlier discussion regarding master numbers. It is the lower levels of mastery of the 11, 22, and 33 that are most within reach of humanity at our current level of enlightenment. It is therefore the 1, 2, and 3 that will tend to dominate the numerology profiles of today's living masters.

Another reason why 1, 2, and 3 appear so often in very accomplished profiles goes right back to the base-12 number system itself. Recall that it is the factors of 2 and 3 upon which base-12 is built and which provides its superior versatility and divisibility for being expressed in many potential ways. So, when a soul incarnates into a particularly high-potential life, it will typically include the 1, 2, and 3 in various combinations as that offers the greatest vibrational flexibility in achieving that scope of potential.

Sample Meanings of Select Words

I find it very revealing to work out the numerology of words with significant meaning to us personally and collectively. Following is a sampling of various words, along with their traditional meaning and vibrational meaning in base-12 numerology. Turn to page 183 for the word *numerology* itself.

Bird: Feathered master of flight.

$2 + 9 + 9 + 4 = 2 \times 12 + 0 = \mathbf{20/2}$ = At home on land or air (2) through duality (2) of potential (0)

Buddha: An ascended master who illuminated the way for humanity.

$2 + 3 + 4 + 4 + 8 + 1 = 1x12 + \underline{10} = \mathbf{110/11}$ = Illumination (**11**) through new beginnings (1) of awareness (**10**)

Business: Exchange of goods and services for remuneration.

$2 + 3 + 1 + 9 + 5 + 5 + 1 + 1 = 2x12 + 3 = \mathbf{23/5}$ (same vibration as *money*) = Transformation of resources into goods and services (5) by balancing supply with demand (2) of the market (3)

Carbon: The fundamental element upon which all organic life is built.

$3 + 1 + 9 + 2 + 6 + 5 = 2x12 + 2 = \mathbf{master\ number\ 22}$ = Mastery of duality, master builder

Cat: Furry family member that expresses love, on their terms.

$3 + 1 + 2 = \mathbf{6}$ = Love (6)

Consciousness: Change in perspective as to the nature of self.

$3 + 6 + 5 + 1 + 3 + 9 + 6 + 3 + 1 + 5 + 5 + 1 + 1 = 4x12 + 1 = \mathbf{41/5} =$ Change (5) in nature (4) of self (1)

Cubic Zirconia: A new cubic crystalline material used as synthetic diamond.

$(3 + 3 + 2 + 9 + 3) + (8 + 9 + 9 + 3 + 6 + 5 + 9 + 1) = (1x12 + 8) + (4x12 + 2) = 18/9 + 42/6 = 9 + 6 = 1x12 + 3 = \mathbf{13/4}$ = Structural stability (4) through a new (1) cubic material (3), or relationship stability (4) through a new beginning (1) of engagement (3)...then relationship *instability* (4) when they discover (1) they've been tricked (3) by a fake diamond!

Dance: Harmony of movement.

$4 + 1 + 5 + 3 + 5 = 1x12 + 6 = \mathbf{16/7}$ = Spiritual truth (7) through new beginnings (1) of harmony (6)

Death: The end of physical life and return to spirit.

$4 + 5 + 1 + 2 + 8 = 1x12 + 8 = \mathbf{18/9}$ = Completion (9) through new beginning (1) of manifestation and abundance (8)

Diamond: An extremely hard and brilliant natural crystalline material made from carbon.

4 + 9 + 1 + 4 + 6 + 5 + 4 = 2x12 + 9 = 29/<u>11</u> = **<u>11</u>** = Illumination (<u>11</u>) through the duality (2) of completion (9) ... and brilliant symbol (<u>11</u>) of the commitment (2) of marriage (9)

Dog: Furry friend that expresses love and always wants to play.

4 + 6 + 7 = 1x12 + 5 = **15/6** = Love (6) through new beginnings (1) of change (5)

Energy: Transformation through vibration.

5 + 5 + 5 + 9 + 7 + 7 = 3x12 + 2 = **32/5** = Change (5) through the catalyst (3) of duality (2)

Evolve: To adapt and grow through exposure to the environment.

5 + 4 + 6 + 3 + 4 + 5 = 2x12 + 3 = **23/5** = Change (5) through the duality (2) of catalysts (3)

Fear: Anxiety of expecting the worst to happen.

6 + 5 + 1 + 9 = 1x12 + 9 = **19/<u>10</u>** = Expecting (<u>10</u>) what is started (1) will fail (9)

Fibonacci: The pattern of regeneration and growth in nature.

6 + 9 + 2 + 6 + 5 + 1 + 3 + 3 + 9 = 3x12 + 8 = **38/<u>11</u>** = Illumination (<u>11</u>) through the catalyst (3) of manifestation (8)

God: Love expressing and experiencing itself in infinitely diverse ways.

7 + 6 + 4 = 1x12 + 5 = **15/6** = Love (6) through new beginnings (1) of change (5)

H_2O: The molecular structure of water.

8 + 8 + 6 = 1x12 + 10 = **1<u>10</u>/<u>11</u>** (same as *water*)

Humane Society: Organization dedicated to the humane treatment of animals.

$(8 + 3 + 4 + 1 + 5 + 5) + (1 + 6 + 3 + 9 + 5 + 2 + 7) = (2x12 + 2) + (2x12 + 9) = 22 + 29/\underline{11} = 3x12 + 1 = \mathbf{31/4} =$ Structure, stability and safety for animals (4) as a catalyst (3) of new beginnings (1)

Jesus: An ascended master who illuminated the way for humanity.

$1 + 5 + 1 + 3 + 1 = \mathbf{\underline{11}} =$ Illumination

Kindness: Consideration for helping others.

$2 + 9 + 5 + 4 + 5 + 5 + 1 + 1 = 2x12 + 8 = \mathbf{28/\underline{10}} =$ Consideration for others (\underline{10}) through sharing (2) of abundance (8)

Life: Beginning of self-sustaining existence.

$3 + 9 + 6 + 5 = 1x12 + \underline{11} = 1x12 + 0 = \mathbf{10/1} =$ New beginnings (1) through start (1) of potential (0)

Llewellyn: Leading global publisher of books for body, mind, and spirit.

$3 + 3 + 5 + 5 + 5 + 3 + 3 + 7 + 5 = 3x12 + 3 = \mathbf{master\ number\ 33} =$ Master catalyst, healer, and teacher

Love: Our divine nature and the essence of All That Is.

$3 + 6 + 4 + 5 = 1x12 + 6 = \mathbf{16/7} =$ Spiritual truth (7) through new beginnings (1) of love (6)

Man: Male human with conscious awareness.

$4 + 1 + 5 = \mathbf{\underline{10}} =$ Awareness

Money: Currency traded in exchange for goods and services.

$4 + 6 + 5 + 5 + 7 = 2x12 + 3 = \mathbf{23/5} =$ Change (5) through the duality (2) of the catalyst (3), or an agent of change (5) in a positive or negative (2) way (3)

Nobel Peace Prize: An award that honors individual contributions to world peace.

$(5 + 6 + 2 + 5 + 3) + (7 + 5 + 1 + 3 + 5) + (7 + 9 + 9 + 8 + 5) = (1x12 + 9) + (1x12 + 9) + (3x12 + 2) = 19/\underline{10} + 19/\underline{10} + 32/5 = \underline{10} + \underline{10} + 5 = 2x12$

+ 1 = **21/3** = Catalyst honoring (3) exemplary peacekeeping efforts (2) by individuals (1)

Numerology: Truth revealed through the vibrational language of numbers.

5 + 3 + 4 + 5 + 9 + 6 + 3 + 6 + 7 + 7 = 4x12 + 7 = **47/11** = Illumination (11) through the structure (4) of knowledge and truth (7)

Oxygen: The fundamental element that is the catalyst of all life.

6 + 6 + 7 + 7 + 5 + 5 = 3x12 + 0 = **30/3** = Catalyst (3) through the catalyst (3) of potential (0)

Peace: Putting an end to conflict.

7 + 5 + 1 + 3 + 5 = 1x12 + 9 = **19/10** = Awareness (10) through new beginnings (1) of completion (9)

Prime: The most basic units from which everything is created.

7 + 9 + 9 + 4 + 5 = 2x12 + 10 = 1x12 + 0 = **10/1** = New beginnings (1) through unit (1) of potential (0)

Reincarnation: Cycle of spirit returning to physical form to gain experience.

9 + 5 + 9 + 5 + 3 + 1 + 9 + 5 + 1 + 2 + 9 + 6 + 5 = 69 = 5x12 + 9 = 59 = 1x12 + 2 = **12/3** = Catalyst for growth (3) through new beginnings (1) of physical-spiritual duality (2)

Society for the Prevention of Cruelty to Animals (SPCA): Organization dedicated to the humane treatment of animals.

(1 + 6 + 3 + 9 + 5 + 2 + 7) + (6 + 6 + 9) + (2 + 8 + 5) + (7 + 9 + 5 + 4 + 5 + 5 + 2 + 9 + 6 + 5) + (6 + 6) + (3 + 9 + 3 + 5 + 3 + 2 + 7) + (2 + 6) + (1 + 5 + 9 + 4 + 1 + 3 + 1) = (2x12 + 9) + (1x12 + 9) + (1x12 + 3) + (4x12 + 9) + (1x12 + 0) + (2x12 + 8) + 8 + (2x12 + 0) = 29/11 + 19/10 + 13/4 + (49/1x12 + 1/11) + 10/1 + 28/10 + 8 + 20/2 = 11 + 10 + 4 + 11 + 1 + 10 + 8 + 2 = 4x12 + 11 = 411 = 4 + 11 = 1x12 + 3 = **13/4** = Structure, stability and safety for animals (4) by taking lead role (1) in changing attitudes (3)

Soul: Enlightened higher self.

$1 + 6 + 3 + 3 = 1x12 + 1 = $ **master number 11** $ = $ Mastery of self

Team: People working together as one.

$2 + 5 + 1 + 4 = 1x12 + 0 = $ **10/1** $ = $ United (1) in new beginnings (1) of potential (0)

The Declaration of Independence: The statement of independence made by the thirteen American colonies from British rule on July 4, 1776.

$(2 + 8 + 5) + (4 + 5 + 3 + 3 + 1 + 9 + 1 + 2 + 9 + 6 + 5) + (6 + 6) + (9 + 5 + 4 + 5 + 7 + 5 + 5 + 4 + 5 + 5 + 3 + 5) = (1x12 + 3/13/4) + (4x12 + 0/40/4) + (1x12 + 0/10/1) + (5x12 + 2/52/7) = 4 + 4 + 1 + 7 = 1x12 + 4 = $ **14/5** $ = $ Freedom (5) through new beginnings (1) of structure and stability (4)

Note: The date of July 4, 1776, has the same 14/5 vibration as the declaration itself, in both base-12 and base-10 (base-12: $7 + 4 + 1040/5 = 7 + 4 + 5 = 1x12 + 4 = 14/5$; base-10: $7 + 4 + 1776/21/3 = 7 + 4 + 3 = 14/5$).

Twelve: Nature's fundamental cycle for creating balance through vibrational potential.

$2 + 5 + 5 + 3 + 4 + 5 = 2x12 + 0 = $ **20/2** $ = $ Duality and balance (2) through vibrational (2) cycles of potential (0)

United Nations: International organization promoting global cooperation and order.

$(3 + 5 + 9 + 2 + 5 + 4) + (5 + 1 + 2 + 9 + 6 + 5 + 1) = (2x12 + 4) + (2x12 + 5) = 24/6 + 25/7 = 6 + 7 = 1x12 + 1 = $ **master number 11** $ = $ Mastery of self as a global collective

Vet: Animal doctor or retired member of the military.

$4 + 5 + 2 = $ **<u>11</u>** $ = $ Illumination

War: Violent force asserted on another.

$5 + 1 + 9 = 1x12 + 3 = $ **13/4** $ = $ Destruction (4) through indiscriminate (1) force (3)

Water: The liquid form of H_2O that enables life to begin.

$5 + 1 + 2 + 5 + 9 = 1\text{x}12 + 10 = \mathbf{1\underline{10}/\underline{11}}$ = Illumination, innovation, and clarity ($\underline{11}$)

Woman: Female human with conscious awareness and who can bear children.

$5 + 6 + 4 + 1 + 5 = 1\text{x}12 + 9 = \mathbf{19/\underline{10}}$ = Awareness ($\underline{10}$) through new beginnings (1) of completion (9)

Appendix:
YOUR BASE-12
NUMEROLOGY ROAD MAP

Birth Name: _____ _____ _____
                          first   *middle*   *last*

Current Name: _____ _____
                           first   *last*

Birth Date: _____ _____ _____
                           month   *day*   *year*

Numerology is based on the principle that everything is energy and has a vibrational character, including numbers, letters and words. My birth date and birth name are the personal vibrational signature I chose for this life. *My birth date reveals what I am here to learn* and the various cycles I will experience along the way, while *my birth name says who I am and how I express myself.* Together, they are the compass heading of my life. The specific choices I make and route I take are up to me, but my vibrational signature will always help keep me on course.

The vibrational "road map" I have chosen for this journey is revealed in my base-12 numerology, where every experience, relationship, or incarnation follows a universal cycle of twelve vibrational themes, from the 0 of potential to the 11 of illumination. How fully I explore each experience determines how fully I may learn the lessons contained within.

Calculation Worksheet

My Base-12 Numerology Road Map and all the insights it reveals about me are based upon my eight forecasting numbers and eight personality numbers calculated below.

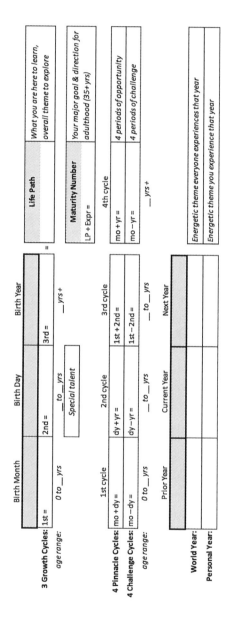

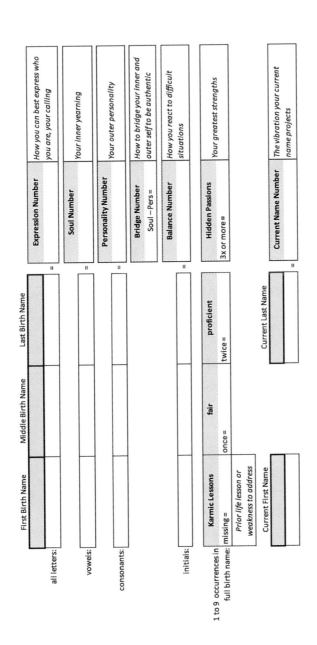

	First Birth Name	Middle Birth Name	Last Birth Name		
all letters:				=	**Expression Number** — *How you can best express who you are, your calling*
vowels:				=	**Soul Number** — *Your inner yearning*
consonants:				=	**Personality Number** — *Your outer personality*
				=	**Bridge Number** Soul – Pers = — *How to bridge your inner and outer self to be authentic*
initials:				=	**Balance Number** — *How you react to difficult situations*

Karmic Lessons	fair	proficient	**Hidden Passions** — *Your greatest strengths*
1 to 9 occurrences in full birth name: missing =	once =	twice =	3x or more =
Prior life lesson or weakness to address			

Current First Name	Current Last Name		
		=	**Current Name Number** — *The vibration your current name projects*

0	1	2	3	4	5	6	7	8	9	10	11		11	22	33
Potential	A	B	C	D	E	F	G	H	I	Awareness	Illumination		Mastery of Self	Mastery of Duality	Master of Catalyst
	J	K	L	M	N	O	P	Q	R						
	S	T	U	V	W	X	Y	Z							
New Beginnings	Duality	Catalyst	Structure	Change	Love	Truth	Manifestation	Completion							

Table 7. Number and Letter Meanings

Forecasting Numbers from My Birth Date: "My Path"

My *life path* (based on my birth date) is the overall theme and major lessons I have chosen to explore and involves learning about _____. This life path indicates I will learn about the theme of _____ through experiences that teach me about _____

_____.

I will experience this theme over *three growth cycles,* each with its own timing and focus:

1. My *first growth cycle* (based on my birth month) will last roughly from birth to age ___ with a focus on the ___ theme of _____
   _____.

2. My *second growth cycle* (birth day) will last about 27 years, from age _____
   to _____ years and will focus on the ___ theme of _____
   _____. Also called my *birth day number,* this is a special talent I possess to help me navigate my life path.

3. My *third growth cycle* (birth year) will last from about age ___ to the rest of my life, with a focus on the ___ theme of _____
   _____.

There are two other types of cycles generated from my birth date; *four pinnacle cycles* that bring periods of opportunity and *four challenge cycles* that present challenges to overcome in pursuing those opportunities:

1. My *first pinnacle cycle* (birth month + birth day) will occur from birth to age ____ bringing opportunities involving the _____ theme of _____ _____. But to take advantage of this, I need to overcome my *first challenge cycle* theme (birth month - day) of _____ involving challenges of _____ _____.

2. My *second pinnacle cycle* (birth day + birth year) will last 9 years from age _____ to _____ with opportunities involving the _____ theme of _____ _____.

3. But to take advantage of this, I need to overcome my *second challenge cycle* theme (birth day—birth year) of _____ involving challenges of _____ _____.

4. My *third pinnacle cycle* (first pinnacle + second pinnacle) will last another 9 years from age ____ to ___, with opportunities involving the _____ theme of _____. But to take advantage of this, I need to overcome my *third challenge cycle* theme (first challenge—second challenge) of _____ involving challenges of _____ _____ _____.

5. My *fourth pinnacle cycle* (birth month + year) will last from age ____ through the rest of my life, with opportunities involving the _____ of _____. But to take advantage of this, I need to overcome my *fourth challenge cycle* (birth month—birth year) of _____ which involves challenges of _____ _____.

191

My *maturity number* is the sum of my life path and expression number and indicates the main direction for the second half of my life (after thirty-five). As my maturity number is _____,

I will focus on _____

_____

_____.

Each year also has its own energetic theme that influences our own personal vibe during the full twelve months. The *world year* affects everyone with the same overall theme, while our *personal year* (year of interest + birth month + birth day) is how we personally feel that year's effect. Following are those numbers for last year, this year and next year:

  + Last year, _____, was a ___ *world year* of _____.
    For me, it was a ___ *personal year* of _____.

  + This year, _____, is a ___ *world year* of _____.
    For me, it is a ___ *personal year* of _____.

  + Next year, _____, will be a ___ *world year* of _____.
    For me, it will be a ___ *personal year* of _____.

Personality Numbers from My Birth Name: "Who I Am"

My birth name reveals that my *expression number* is _____. This means that I can best express my true self and potential in areas involving _____

_____

_____.

The vowels of my birth name reveal my *soul number*, my soul's inner yearning. As my soul number is _____, my inner yearning is for _____

_____

_____.

Likewise, the consonants in my birth name give my *personality number*, my outer personality of how I am perceived by others. The energy I project is the _____ vibration of _____ _____.

The difference between my soul and personality numbers is my *bridge number*. This indicates how I can adjust my outer behaviour (personality) to better align with how I see myself (soul), how to be perceived as authentic. My bridge number is _____, so embodying the positive qualities of _____ _____ _____ reveals my soul's true nature.

How I react in difficult situations is my *balance number* and is given by the first initials of my birth name. My balance number is ____, so under pressure I tend to exhibit _____ _____ _____.

The number of times each letter-number energy from 1 to 9 appears in my birth name indicates my relative strengths and weaknesses at this point in my soul's development. Those appearing three or more times are considered my *hidden passions*, my strengths. For me, these include _____ _____. As such, I have the positive qualities of _____ _____ _____ _____.

Any letter-number missing from my birth name is a *karmic lesson* and high-lights a specific weakness or unresolved lesson carried over from my prior lives. By choosing a birth name missing the letter vibration of my karmic lesson(s), I will feel its absence and the need to work at it as a priority for this life. My karmic lesson(s) is _____, which involves learning to be

_____

_____.

The last of the numbers in my Base-12 Numerology Road Map is my *current name number*. Although my full birth name (Expression number) reflects who I truly am, the current name I use can adjust that vibration and the energy it projects.

My current name of _____

projects the _____ vibration of _____

_____.

RECOMMENDED READING

Braden, Gregg. *The Divine Matrix*. Carlsbad, CA: Hay House, 2007.

Carroll, Lee. *The Twelve Layers of DNA*. Sedona, AZ: Platinum Publishing House, 2010.

Decoz, Hans, and Tom Monte. *Numerology*. New York: Penguin Group, 1994.

Hicks, Esther, and Jerry Hicks. *The Law of Attraction*. Carlsbad, CA: Hay House, 2006.

Lipton, Bruce. *The Biology of Belief*. Carlsbad, CA: Hay House, 2005.

Peirce, Penney. *Frequency*. New York: Atria Books/Beyond Words Publishing, 2009.

Roberts, Jane. *Seth Speaks*. San Rafael, CA: Amber-Allen Publishing, 1972.

Rother, Steve. *Re-member*. Poway, CA: Lightworker, 2000.

To Write to the Author

If you wish to contact the author or would like more information about this book, please write to the author in care of Llewellyn Worldwide Ltd. and we will forward your request. Both the author and the publisher appreciate hearing from you and learning of your enjoyment of this book and how it has helped you. Llewellyn Worldwide Ltd. cannot guarantee that every letter written to the author can be answered, but all will be forwarded. Please write to:

Michael Smith
℅ Llewellyn Worldwide
2143 Wooddale Drive
Woodbury, MN 55125-2989

Please enclose a self-addressed stamped envelope for reply,
or $1.00 to cover costs. If outside the U.S.A., enclose
an international postal reply coupon.

Many of Llewellyn's authors have websites with additional information and resources. For more information, please visit our website at http://www.llewellyn .com.

GET MORE AT LLEWELLYN.COM

Visit us online to browse hundreds of our books and decks, plus sign up to receive our e-newsletters and exclusive online offers.

• Free tarot readings • Spell-a-Day • Moon phases

• Recipes, spells, and tips • Blogs • Encyclopedia

• Author interviews, articles, and upcoming events

GET SOCIAL WITH LLEWELLYN

Find us on  @LlewellynBooks

www.Facebook.com/LlewellynBooks

GET BOOKS AT LLEWELLYN

LLEWELLYN ORDERING INFORMATION

 Order online: Visit our website at www.llewellyn.com to select your books and place an order on our secure server.

 Order by phone:
• Call toll free within the US at 1-877-NEW-WRLD (1-877-639-9753)
• We accept VISA, MasterCard, American Express, and Discover.

 Order by mail:
Send the full price of your order (MN residents add 6.875% sales tax) in US funds plus postage and handling to: Llewellyn Worldwide, 2143 Wooddale Drive, Woodbury, MN 55125-2989

POSTAGE AND HANDLING

STANDARD (US):(Please allow 12 business days)
$30.00 and under, add $6.00.
$30.01 and over, FREE SHIPPING.

CANADA:
We cannot ship to Canada. Please shop your local bookstore or Amazon Canada.

INTERNATIONAL:
Customers pay the actual shipping cost to the final destination, which includes tracking information.

Visit us online for more shipping options. Prices subject to change.

FREE CATALOG!

To order, call
1-877-
NEW-WRLD
ext. 8236
or visit our
website